CHICANO
HOMELAND

CHICANO HOMELAND

The Movement in East Los Angeles
for Mexican American
Power, Justice, and Equality

Louis R. Negrete

ISBN: 1519355262
ISBN 13: 9781519355263

Table of Contents

Introduction

Something astonishing was happening at the school.

On Friday, March 1, 1968, I was driving my car along Eastern Avenue in front of Woodrow Wilson High School in El Sereno, California, when a crowd of young students ran across the street, closely chased by Los Angeles police cars with loudspeakers ordering them to return to campus.

They didn't.

I parked my car and watched the students vacate the school at an ever-increasing pace, ignoring the demands and threats of the authorities. I saw one student jump over the school fence and run up an adjacent hill, chased by black and white police cars. Students on campus cheered loudly at the entertaining spectacle of police ineffectively chasing students. When I asked what was going on, one girl told me that running away from school was due to cancellation of a popular student play by the school principal. As a result, hundreds of students on campus refused to attend class and sat on bleachers next to the football field until school dismissed.

I left amazed. At the time, I served as Director of Project Head Start for the Council of Mexican American Affairs headquartered in Lincoln Heights. I was aware of discontent within the Chicano community regarding education of their children and other longstanding complaints, but I had never seen that form of student protest, and wrongly thought I would never see anything like it again.

The following Tuesday, I happened to be driving along North Broadway in front of Abraham Lincoln High School in Lincoln Heights when I saw another large crowd of students run out of the school to the sidewalk, where they formed a march and carried posters that demanded better schools. It was an unforgettable sight. I had never seen any organized protest like this by teenage students. I later found out that students had also walked out at James A. Garfield High School in unincorporated East Los Angeles and Theodore Roosevelt High School in Boyle Heights.

That's when I realized that something big was going on, something never seen before in Los Angeles or possibly the nation. These young people promoted the slogan "Walk Out Now or Drop Out Tomorrow," meaning that protest was necessary to force the schools to teach.

I felt a sense of pride that the students themselves were demanding better schools. To my thinking, their requests were reasonable: a reduced class size, new schools with Mexican names, Spanish speaking counselors, improved curricula, expanded library facilities, improved building facilities, and fair enforcement of school rules. But school officials ignored the student demands, and this set the stage for the first Mexican American high school student strike in the nation. The students called their strike the "walkouts" or "blowouts."[1]

During the walkouts, outraged school officials summoned the police, who arrested several teenage students on the picket line. I saw a young male absorb a blow from a police baton while he stood between a student protester and an angry policeman in front of Roosevelt High School in Boyle Heights. Parents of protesting students charged police brutality and, to make certain they were heard, held a sit-in of their own at the office of the District Attorney.

These protests inspired me. I felt the urge to become more assertive in my own opposition to anti-Mexican racism. The student walkouts added fuel to the fire not only for me but for hundreds of other activists to become more visible in opposing racism wherever it occurred. Those of us who worked in the professions, business, and non-profits shared concerns about social and economic conditions in our neighborhoods, our "barrios." Student shouts of "Chicano Power" at gatherings after the walkouts generated energy and passion for justice, especially in the predominantly Latino neighborhoods of El Sereno, Lincoln Heights, Boyle Heights, and unincorporated East Los Angeles.

The protests seemed to work. The high school walkouts sparked energetic political activism in East Los Angeles. In 1968, about a week after the walkouts, an emergency committee of Mexican American activists endorsed the student demands and called for talks between the school board and striking students.[2] This set in place a major confrontation between the Chicano community and the Los Angles school board.

It was a turning point that none of us had seen coming, and all of us today can mark something in our history from that time.

What follows is description of how the Chicano movement became part of the strong winds of civil discontent that swept across the nation. Thousands of people, mostly anonymous, participated in movement events like members of a liberating army. Chicano rhetoric connected protest events and concepts with each other and attracted large numbers of men and women. We felt our community come together in ways it never had before. By our numbers, we were creating new opportunities and awareness

I was an early beneficiary of these changes. Shortly after the walkouts began, I was offered an opportunity to become a member of the founding faculty of the new Department of Mexican American Studies at California State University, Los Angeles. In the years that followed, the 1960's and 1970's, I became both an observer and a participant of the Chicano movement for power in East Los Angeles, and I experienced first-hand the Chicano part of the American Civil Rights Movement.

The focus of this book is on creating an overview and description of Chicano movement actions, meetings, groups, rhetoric, and historic events as they unfolded. Other worthy academic books focused on individual organizations or leaders. I focus on a wide range of movement events without promoting any single ideological perspective.

Many different forms of actions with different goals occurred at the same time, so a chronological approach seems most appropriate to map out the evolution of the movement. While I concentrate on the 1960's and 1970's, I touch upon roots going back to the native Mexican population, then bring things into the present with a projection of what our future may look like.

To create our future, it is important to know and understand our history. To the best of my recollection, notes, and research, this how the movement happened in East Los Angeles for Mexican American power, justice and equality.

Chapter 1

Roots of Activism

Social movements have unseen beginnings that lead to important forms of political action. In East Los Angeles, some activists traced the origins of the Chicano movement to Aztec resistance against the Spanish invasion of Mexico. Others said the movement started over smoldering resentment over the loss of the U.S. Southwest after the U.S. War with Mexico. Still other activists pointed to a legacy of the Mexican Revolution of 1910.

But the roots of the movement can also be traced to a series of events closer to home. In Los Angeles during World War II, U.S. sailors assisted by police officers attacked young Chicanos on the streets in downtown Los Angeles, Lincoln Heights, and Watts. The assaults in June, 1943, became known in the media as the Zoot Suit Riots. The media blamed Chicano youth for street confrontations with the sailors, but in truth the confrontations should have been called "The Sailor Riots."

These riots started after a street fight between sailors and young Chicano men and teenagers. The sailors and media identified Chicano youth in public by their pachuco dress style: baggy pants tied tight around the ankles. The media exaggerated a sinister anti-social meaning to the dress style of Chicanos on the streets. This racial exaggeration occurred at the same time that strong anti-Japanese public attitudes existed due to the attack on Pearl Harbor, which led to the creation of internment camps where Japanese families were segregated from

1

American society. Mexicans were likewise seen as inferior, especially if they dressed pachuco style.

When I was nine years old, I saw my uncle chased down 103rd Street in Watts by a small group of sailors in uniform who were guarded by Los Angeles city policemen. My uncle ran into the front of the Largo Theater near Wilmington Avenue and out the back door. The sailors were not allowed to enter the theater in order to protect movie customers who did not know what was going outside. We all noticed that the sailors and police were white and the escaping pachuchos were Mexican American. Afterwards, my parents warned me and my cousins to be watchful of sailors or policemen, and to always come straight home.

Even as the media considered Pachucos as unpatriotic and un-American, Chicanos distinguished themselves in military service to the United States. They fought in the military in both Europe and the Pacific, earning more Medals of Honor than any other racial group during World War II. [1]

After the war, Mexican American veterans in Los Angeles turned their attention away from the horrors of war. They faced what seemed to be an unlimited future of peace, prosperity, and social progress shared by the entire nation. The federal government and U.S. corporations seemed unstoppable, ready to dominate world commerce and politics through near perfection of military power and technological innovation. The future looked bright and prosperous.

Returning Mexican American veterans -- like my three uncles, all of whom were Honorably Discharged from the army -- had great expectations. They envisioned equal opportunity that would provide them with the American Dream of a home for every family, stable job, good schools for their children, and quiet neighborhoods. They would no longer be treated like second class citizens.

These returning veterans boldly pursued full entitlement to benefits of democracy and economic opportunity. Many of them attended college under the 1944 GI Bill of Rights that supported veterans to receive a higher education. They began to form a noticeable Mexican American middle class as attorneys, social workers, teachers, and business owners.

These optimistic times also found large numbers of Mexican American veterans employed in factories for automobiles, rubber goods, refrigerators, steel, and the canning industry that were needed to satisfy a growing world consumer demand for U.S. products. Veterans also joined labor unions, where they learned organizational skills such as the use of prepared agendas, published minutes, and newsletters. They helped forge community links with organized labor and with larger political movements in Southern California.

At first, the alliance between labor and the Mexican American community was more helpful to labor than to the community. Organized labor's help was sporadic and dealt mostly with problems aligned with the union's agenda. Thus, in spite of help from labor unions, a political power vacuum continued to exist in the Mexican American community.[2]

Meanwhile, a segment of Mexican Americans in Southern California began to form a more visible presence in local politics. New businesses, better jobs, and higher incomes led to increased civic activism and opportunities for a sharper articulation of community concerns. In 1945, Mexican American activists won the Mendez v. Westminster court decision that declared racially segregated public schools in California unconstitutional.[3]

Lawyers became prime actors in defense of local communities. In 1959, attorneys formed the Mexican American Bar Association to defend the civil rights of Mexican Americans in Los Angeles. But even though legal victories advanced entitlement to civil rights, a larger sector of the Mexican American people remained powerless, depending upon legal experts for redress of grievances.

Returning veterans also saw a big increase in the Mexican American population in Los Angeles. Large numbers of new immigrants from Mexico settled in the city, learned to speak English, and participated in the city social life. War veterans, community and labor union activists, and recent immigrants joined civic groups like the League of United Latin American Citizens (LULAC), the Unity Leagues, the Council of Mexican American Affairs (CMAA), the American GI Forum, and the Community Service Organization (CSO) that advocated civil rights for Mexican Americans.[4]

The CSO, formed initially with leadership of Mexican American war veterans,[5] serves as an example of early effective Mexican American civic group organizing. The CSO sought to reduce the impact of poverty and political disenfranchisement, and to defend immigrants. Organized with the help of Fred Ross, staff organizer for the Industrial Areas Foundation (IAF) in 1947, the CSO became the largest community-based political organization in East Los Angeles. CSO membership consisted mostly of working class, immigrant, and Spanish speaking families. The group conducted voter registration drives and emphasized training new community organizers as a major goal. Most significantly, CSO trained both Cesar Chavez, who was a U.S. Navy veteran, and Dolores Huerta, who together went on to found the United Farm Workers Union (UFW).

Through the CSO, volunteer teachers taught English language and citizenship classes in Spanish to immigrants. By November of 1962, almost everyone interested in applying for citizenship in Spanish had been prepared for the examination.[6]

With support of the CSO, Edward R. Roybal, a highly respected Mexican American community activist, ran for a seat on the Los Angeles City Council in 1947. He lost. But in 1949, on his second try, the CSO played a prominent role in his election. A cross-town multiracial coalition, including the CSO and other groups in the East side, made the difference in a city council district where Mexican American voters made up less than a third of the votes cast. Led by Tony Rios and Ursula Gutierrez, this victory by the CSO became the most prominent win in newly emerging Mexican American civic group politics.

Eventually, the CSO began to focus more on fundraising for scholarships, credit unions for self-help, and referral of police abuse complaints to attorneys. It was then that Cesar Chavez, Dolores Huerta, and other leaders resigned from the CSO and later formed the United Farm Workers (UFW).[7] The CSO, however, continued to defend immigrant rights along with other civic groups in the 1950's, as it continues to do to this day.

Today, Los Angeles remains central to Mexican American participation to state and national politics.[8] [9] [10] [11] [12] The city has the largest number of Mexican Americans in the country. Cultural events like participation in church or celebration of the 16th of September as Mexican independence from Spain bring families together. They also celebrate the 5th of May as Cinco de Mayo to remember the victory of a small Mexican contingent over a larger French force in Puebla in 1862. The concept is that a more powerful enemy can be defeated -- a concept that has fueled and supported our movement for equality all along.

Chapter 2

The Fifties

The Fifties affected movement activists in Los Angeles in major ways. This was the decade when ambitious and optimistic young people everywhere pursued higher education; sought to learn skills for challenging careers in large, complex organizations in the public and private sectors; when television sets became basic home furniture; and when the U.S. Supreme Court followed the California legal precedent and ruled that "separate but equal" school segregation was unconstitutional.

It was also a time of controversy, with major, sometimes contradictory, turns in political and social life. This was the decade when President Dwight D. Eisenhower committed U.S. troops to fight a communist takeover in Korea and to stop world communism; when U.S. Senator Joseph McCarthy conducted his infamous "witch hunt" for communists in America; and when Fidel Castro led his victorious troops into Havana. Constant media reports on activities of the nearby communist country of Cuba kept the threat of communism alive as a possible attraction of activist supporters, especially in Spanish speaking communities like Los Angeles.

During this changing and generally prosperous decade, Mexican Americans in Los Angeles began to divide into a majority of low income families and a smaller number of middle class families. War veterans continued to pursue opportunities for college and became educators, social workers, lawyers, and small business owners. Others attended technical schools for training as automobile mechanics, plumbers, and electricians.

Some Mexican Americans used small loans from banks to move up in financial and social status. During this time, my mother insisted that I attend American Barber College downtown after high school to keep me away from my group of friends, who she considered a negative influence. I then became a barber, which made it possible for me to pay for my college education.

A small but important number of Mexican American families broke out of poverty. They moved out of poor neighborhoods, known as the barrios -- areas such as Watts, Willowbrook, and Boyle Heights -- to more conventional areas like Montebello, Monterey Park, and La Puente. Families were determined to live in better neighborhoods with better schools. As they shifted from low to middle class lifestyles, they became the main boosters of a civic group approach to politics.

In Los Angeles, however, most Mexican American families remained in racially segregated low income neighborhoods east and south of downtown. That was my family's story. In these neighborhoods, we had to deal not only with neglect by the city government but with regular abuse by police.

I experienced police abuse as a teenager growing up in Watts. One night, during an asthma attack at home, I fell and hit my head on a TV set. I walked unseen out the front door in a daze and was having difficulty breathing. Two police officers stopped me near the corner of Holmes Avenue and 92nd Street. They asked me questions I did not properly answer because I was still dazed. They took me into custody and later my parents picked me up off a cot at the police station. I had bruises on my chest and back, but not on my face.

In the following day, my parents noticed a police car slowly pass in front of our home. This caused them to fear I would get beaten up again, so they rented a room for me across town in El Sereno, near the intersection of Van Horne and Huntington Drive. I stayed in the room for several weeks and took the daily bus to my classes at Cathedral High School. I returned home after the police car stopped cruising in front of our house. (In spite of this, I respect police officers, but understand a lingering community mistrust of law enforcement.)

Racial discrimination in employment and housing, as well as inferior public schools contributed to persistent poverty and joblessness. It kept Mexican Americans socially apart from the rest of society. When upwardly mobile families moved out of the inner city, they removed themselves as "success models" for the community. They left behind more recent immigrant, less advantaged, and less financially stable families. A low income Chicano urban class began to form.

Even the physical shape of the old neighborhoods changed in the Fifties. New freeways and concrete slabs split up neighborhoods, reduced the size of local parks, destroyed homes, and uprooted families from friends and familiar surroundings. An ambitious urban renewal project removed an entire low income Mexican American neighborhood from Bunker Hill in the downtown area to make way for an office and luxury housing development.

Urban removal had a lasting adverse effect on Chicano voter power. The removal of hundreds of families from old neighborhoods scattered Mexican American voters throughout a larger multi-district area. This made it impossible for Mexican American voters to become a majority in any one district for over forty years and, as a result, land developers and lobbyists continued to dominate local politics.

A lack of jobs, a high casualty rate of Mexican American soldiers in the Korean War, and a sense of political powerlessness all contributed to a lessening of political power and a need for an activist movement. But activists continued a quest for justice through participation in electoral campaigns. They faced usual special interests that dominate electoral politics. In the meantime, they became an identifiable but powerless ethnic group in local and national electoral politics.

Barrio Electoral Politics

During the Fifties, a few Mexican American activists became experts at "barrio politics" attached to elected incumbents, usually liberal Democrats. They worked to deliver the Mexican American vote for

8

favorite politicians, but a traditional ethnic political power broker never emerged to hand out patronage jobs. Visions of old style ethnic politics, like the Italian and Irish political machines back east, never materialized. Independent activist groups in the neighborhoods did not emerge for a more decisive influence in local electoral campaigns. Instead, they placed their hopes for less poverty on campaign promises by favorite office holders.

A few activists became staff members for local elected officials. The best of them worked closely with community groups; the worst become "gate keepers" who kept other activists and community groups at a distance from elected officials.

In 1954, Mexican American activists volunteered to help Los Angeles City Councilman Edward R. Roybal's campaign for Lt. Governor. He lost, but the campaign tightened community involvement in electoral politics. The 1958 losing campaign of Henry Lopez for Secretary of State also focused activists on candidates and campaigns, with a determination to get better organized on a statewide basis.

In 1959, I joined other activists in the formation of the Mexican American Political Association (MAPA). During our founding meetings, activists from throughout the state shared a strong belief that we could change politics in California to end poverty and racism in our communities, and to defend immigrant families. We talked of how our people would obtain good jobs, better schools, and social justice when we elected Mexican American candidates to city, state, and federal offices.

We shared a strong belief that electoral politics would work in our favor to solve community problems. We talked of how Mexican American politicians would bring a new era of social justice. We pledged to organize voters wherever they lived, to work independent of the Democratic and Republican parties and, at the same time, to form voter blocs within both parties to boost Mexican American candidates. We spoke of ourselves as a "sleeping giant" that would one day wake up to smash injustice.

9

In Northern and Southern regional meetings during the formative years, MAPA pledged to organize chapters and run candidates throughout the state in districts with a high number of registered voters with Spanish surnames. But in time, membership in MAPA appealed mostly to activists already involved in electoral politics.

Nonetheless, Democratic and Republican statewide candidates requested an endorsement at MAPA conventions so they could claim they had the support of Mexican American voters. The endorsing convention became a MAPA hallmark and its major contribution to electoral politics.

On a broader scale, Mexican American middle class activists and professionals raised college scholarship funds for successful high school students. They helped serve the working poor with new nonprofit agencies and programs. Social service programs, including state General Relief (GR) and Aid to Families with Dependent Children (AFDC) emerged in local neighborhoods alongside an expanding small business and professional sector. The service providers became better organized and self-sufficient with public and private funding, and they developed strong ties to local communities. A profile of services needed by the poor began to become clearer.

The Fifties ended with worsening national racial problems, a national Civil Rights Movement, and the growing prominence of Rev. Martin Luther King Jr. Protest movements were about to break out in America that would impact on Mexican American politics in Los Angeles.

Chapter 3

The Early Sixties

Events in America during the early 1960's led to the rapid growth of a variety of social movements. The news media publicized communist social movements across the world on a daily basis. These political events had an impact on activist groups in American cities.

Mexican American activists in Los Angeles participated in the great American drama that framed the Sixties, the nomination and election of a U.S. President. The Democratic Party nominating convention, televised nationally from Los Angeles in July, 1960, nominated John F. Kennedy to challenge California native son Richard M. Nixon, the Republican nominee. Both presidential candidates recruited Mexican American volunteers as campaign workers. Hector P. Garcia, a medical doctor and war veteran in Corpus Christi, Texas, organized the multi-state American GI Forum to demand respect for the rights of veterans. He also formed "Viva Kennedy" clubs, a loose network of civic groups in major cities in the Southwest, including Los Angeles.

The well-financed Kennedy campaign also spoke directly to Mexican American voters with Spanish language television and newspapers. Mexican American families responded enthusiastically on Election Day to the young Irish Catholic candidate and his Spanish-speaking wife, Jacqueline. Kennedy barely won the national election by a whisker, but the Mexican American vote was lopsided in his favor.

The size of the Mexican American vote for President Kennedy reinforced hope and expectations that the Kennedy administration would provide some form of liberation from inferior schools, rundown housing, and unaffordable medical bills. But once back in control of the White House, the Democratic Party, like the Republican Party before it, reneged on its piled high campaign promises. The new federal administration continued to ignore the employment and housing needs of the Mexican American people.

Mexican American activists in Los Angeles who worked in the victorious Kennedy campaign became more inspired to develop their own electoral power to get things done. Even though a million of them lived in Los Angeles County at this time, none served on the Los Angles County Board of Supervisors, nor in the State Legislature. They narrowed their quest for electoral power to East Los Angeles, where Mexican Americans were then concentrated. In 1960, MAPA activist Leopoldo Sanchez became the first Mexican American in California elected as a judge when he won election to the Municipal Court in East Los Angeles. In 1965, he was appointed to the Los Angeles Superior Court by then-governor Edmund Brown.

In 1961, activists organized for a vote to incorporate East Los Angeles as a Mexican American city. Resident voters, however, rejected the cityhood measure. Two other incorporation attempts also failed in 1963 and 1974 because they were unable to mobilize sufficient votes for electoral power in a new city. [1] [2] [3]

Mexican American activists spoke openly of support for the more aggressive civil rights protest movement then taking shape in the South. Black students there conducted nonviolent "sit-in" demonstrations in racially segregated places. Students refused to move from white-only restaurants and public buildings. At the same time, small nonviolent interracial groups of activists called "freedom riders" rode segregated buses to challenge segregated bus terminals and rest rooms. They faced terror directly when white mobs savagely attacked them. A whole series of nonviolent challenges and violent responses began the radical

12

youth movement of the Sixties. As a result, the Black struggle organized around Black churches dominated the Civil Rights Movement in America.

By 1962, the U.S. became more involved in the war in Vietnam. President Kennedy authorized limited military assistance for South Vietnam and the first U.S. casualties died there. But in Los Angeles, Mexican American civic groups paid more attention to events closer to home. Possibilities in electoral politics looked better when Los Angeles City Councilman Edward R. Roybal won election to the U.S. Congress from East Los Angeles. But his election that year created a vacuum in city politics for Mexican Americans. No one, even from among his most loyal followers, had been prepared to succeed him as a viable candidate for the city council. As a result, no Mexican American served on the Los Angeles City Council for the next 25 years.

Also in 1962, as the national Civil Rights Movement picked up steam, an alternative independent approach to political power emerged from the lowest paid and most vulnerable Mexican American and immigrant workers in California. Cesar Chavez applied his training and experience with the Community Social Organization (CSO) to organize farm workers into a labor union against powerful California growers. The United Farm Workers Union (UFW) campaign eventually sparked Mexican American militancy throughout the Southwest for civil rights and against poverty.

Late in 1963, the Cuban missile crisis created a national fear of nuclear war with the Soviet Union. A small peace movement began to form, along with an emergent feminist movement. At the same time, the national Civil Rights Movement forged ahead. That August, over 200,000 multiracial activists marched for civil rights in Washington D.C. This marked the occasion of Rev. Martin Luther King's famous "I Have A Dream" speech.

More ominously, Americans saw Buddhist monks on television torch themselves and burn to death to protest the U.S.-supported government in South Vietnam. Then, on November 22, 1963, President

Kennedy was assassinated in Dallas, plunging the nation into deep mourning as Vice President Lyndon B. Johnson became President and vowed to continue U.S. military policy in Southeast Asia.

President Kennedy's assassination, together with the Civil Rights Movement and the peace movement, formed a larger background of simmering unrest. Then, in 1964, a student Free Speech movement at the University of California at Berkeley erupted as a challenge to campus authority, as well as a demand for student self-determination and freedom of speech to oppose the U.S. war policy. University officials called on the California National Guard to suppress the massive student unrest. News of this clash served as an example of what students could do to exercise student power for action on their demands and freedom of expression. Then in July, violent riots broke out in the Black ghettos of four east coast cities. Malcolm X and the Nation of Islam, militant activists for civil rights for all African Americans, became more prominent in national unrest.

The national Civil Rights and anti-war movements continued to gain ground, especially after Rev. Martin Luther King received the Noble Prize for Peace in 1964. But the wheels of war spun faster as President Johnson requested and Congress enacted the Tonkin Gulf Resolution in response to reports of an armed attack on a U.S. vessel near the coast of Vietnam. The President, reelected in 1964, continued to expand the U.S. military presence in Vietnam.

Poverty and Riots

1964 became a "hot summer" of urban unrest and riots in major cities. Class divisions between the rich and poor grew further apart. Low-income families experienced worsening circumstances. Summer riots, increased poverty, and clear racial injustice prompted President Johnson to pledge an expansion of the "Great Society" to reach the poor in America. He launched his own "War on Poverty" with funds set aside to establish federal and local programs for community self-development.

Among the programs begun at this time was Head Start. As expected, the federal money came with strict conditions and much red tape. Eventually, the War on Poverty became a bureaucratic swamp where good intentions sank and disappeared.

As a Head Start director at that time, I discovered that the federal government controlled the War on Poverty by requiring complex regulations, rules, and audits of federally-funded anti-poverty agencies. Nonetheless, hundreds of people found training and employment with federally funded community agencies. Most agencies hired workers from local neighborhoods, but that forced agencies to compete with each other for scarce funds. In Los Angeles, War on Poverty politics degenerated into fierce competition for funds between Black and Mexican American nonprofit service agencies. In-fighting for scarce funds led to replacement of the Economic And Youth Opportunity Agency (EYOA) after seven years of troubled failure in the face of fierce competition for federal money.

The Greater Los Angeles Area Community Action Agency (GLACAA) became the Los Angeles Anti-Poverty agency as of January 1, 1973. This change placed fiscal controls in the hands of the City Treasurer and Controller. The move lessened tension between Blacks and Chicano groups, but competition over funding continued.[4]

In the meantime, poverty persisted in Mexican American neighborhoods. Although Project Head Start succeeded with Spanish speaking families and children, in the end, even hard working anti-poverty workers with good intentions became frustrated with problems linked to poverty. The Los Angeles Times reported how former antipoverty officials accepted work for private management and consulting firms that earned profits from antipoverty efforts.[5] Thus, even government funded agencies had limited success against poverty in racially segregated areas.

Poverty in Los Angeles was concentrated in South Central and East Los Angeles where mostly Black and Mexican American families lived. Today, immigrants from El Salvador, Guatemala, Nicaragua, and Mexico constitute a majority of the people in the South Central area, but in the mid-Sixties, it was clearly a Black neighborhood. Both racially segregated areas had high levels of frustration and anger with poverty, and were ready to explode like dynamite in civil unrest.

The war in Vietnam in the meantime continued to expand. It escalated with direct combat between U.S. Marines and the Viet Cong along with the start of U.S. concentrated air bombing. At the same time, social conditions worsened in Los Angeles for both Mexican Americans and Blacks.

On August 11, 1965, a week after President Johnson signed the Voting Rights Act, community rage blew up in protest when, on a hot summer night, a white California Highway Patrol officer stopped and arrested a Black motorist in South Central Los Angeles. People at the scene reacted angrily. Things got out of control and the Watts Riots began. It was an explosion of deeply felt repressed anger at injustice. The riot resulted in burning, looting, and the death of 34 people, as well as 1,032 people wounded, 3,952 arrests, and $40 million in estimated property damage over a six day period. The Los Angeles police blamed hot weather for the riot, but local residents blamed longtime resentment over lack of jobs, poor schools, and police brutality. [6]

Inquiries after the riot convinced me that a riot could have just as easily erupted in East Los Angeles. Deteriorated social conditions related to inadequate schools and high unemployment made us ripe for a similar explosion of massive spontaneous rage and civil disobedience. But a dramatic triggering event, like a major incident of police brutality, didn't happen there that summer. The California Department of Social Welfare had warned state officials of potential civil unrest in both areas due to massive unemployment, but nobody listened.[7] And so, community outrage continued to build up over unequal social conditions.

Broken Government

The federal government was not responsive to critical problems of the Mexican American working poor. President Johnson's National

Advisory Commission on Civil Disorders investigated the Watts riots as racism between whites and Blacks; it ignored racism against the Mexican American people. As a result, national attention focused on Black poverty and need to alleviate social conditions linked to unemployment in mostly Black areas. The lack of federal government attention to Mexican American poverty forced activists into the politics of competition for scarce government funds for social service and job training programs. Ultimately, both Black and Mexican American nonprofits lost out to the government's "divide and conquer" strategy. Inferior schools and persistent poverty remained in both communities.

During this time, a third of all Mexican American students in the state dropped out of high school before graduation. The high dropout rate correlated to the rate of incarceration in state penal institutions, where almost half of the inmates were of Mexican descent. Over half of all drug addicts were Mexican Americans, and an inordinate high number were unemployed and receiving welfare. Even though Mexican Americans paid ten percent of taxes for the support of public schools, they lacked even one percent of the representation on school boards, trusteeships, or commissions of education in the state. Thus biased IQ tests, inappropriate textbooks, an inadequate curriculum, and unprepared teachers became instruments of discrimination against the Mexican American people.[8]

In 1965, a group of Los Angeles teachers became proactive about inferior schools and formed the Association of Mexican American Educators (AMAE). It worked to improve underfunded and overcrowded schools from inside the school system. The group encouraged parent involvement in the schools and attempted to influence the training of teachers prior to their assignment to schools in Mexican American areas. It made a focused effort to help the public schools improve curricula and teaching methods, but school administrators were not in a receptive mood. In 1974, AMAE sued the Los Angeles public schools for discriminatory practices against Mexican American teachers.[9] Over the years, AMAE became a respected professional organization of teachers and school administrators for an affirmative action agenda.

During this time, years of active opposition ended the government-sponsored *bracero* program that imported Mexican farm workers to this country. U.S. agribusiness used imported farmworkers to break strikes on farms and to block unionization of farm workers. These farmworkers were willing to work for low wages while at the same time fearful of deportation at the hands of growers and the immigration service. Labor organizers and community activists like Ernesto Galarza,[10] the UFW, and a coalition of civil rights, religious, labor and community organizations, worked to defeat this program. Ultimately, agribusiness lost the right to bring farm workers from Mexico into the U.S. The elimination of *braceros* as strikebreakers opened new opportunities for union organizing and added fuel to the UFW campaign to organize California farm workers.[11]

The end of the *bracero* program gave rise to the new Border Industrialization Program (BIP) for economic development of northern Mexico and the U.S. Southwest. The two contiguous areas were to function as one economic region of shared labor, capital, technology, resources, and management techniques.[12] The BIP gave U.S. corporations tax incentives to relocate inside the unorganized low wage labor market in northern Mexico. This dual economic development had a major impact on Los Angeles because thousands of workers attracted to northern Mexico were unable to find employment, so they continued into California for jobs. Because they lacked proper papers, they became known as undocumented workers.

Mexican American civic groups now faced fast-paced changes in social conditions, new social pressures, and an increase in national protest against the Vietnam War, along with persistent racial discrimination. Across the county, activist demands also grew louder for gay and women's liberation. This social protest rolled across America and gained momentum to create a new radical climate for political activism in Los Angeles.

Mexican American activist groups, however, continued to rely mostly on lawyers and legal demands for equal civil rights. In 1968, activists

18

formed the Mexican American Legal Defense and Educational Fund (MALDEF) in San Antonio -- with outreach to Los Angeles -- to defend the civil rights of Latinos. Activists in Los Angeles slowly gave some attention to the growing anti-war national movement. A larger, wider, organized movement for justice was not yet evident.

Chapter 4

The Mid-Sixties

The Plan of Delano

By the mid-Sixties, Chicano movement activists were swamped with news of anti-war protest across the country. U.S. military commanders, convinced of eventual victory, continued to escalate heavy bombing of North Vietnam to keep Saigon under U.S. control. In the summer of 1965, the first large anti-war march took place in Washington D.C., with rhetoric that linked U.S. attacks on North Vietnamese peasants with racist attacks on Blacks in the South. University students held "teach-ins" against the war, against U.S. military intervention in the Dominican Republic, and against higher calls for the military draft. Some students also burned their military draft cards in protest.

At the same time, U.S. business corporations began to face what they called fierce foreign competition. In this competitive labor market, unskilled immigrant workers and Mexican American youth, if employed, found work mostly in sub-minimum wage jobs. Less educated and untrained young people, in particular, faced economic hardship because of the scarcity of jobs. These social circumstances again pointed back to an undeclared crisis of inferior schools, restless youth, and impending social unrest.

An enduring call to militancy reached Los Angeles and the Southwest from Cesar Chavez, who led the United Farm Workers' bitter strike then taking place against California agribusiness. The UFW's *Plan de Delano*, or Plan of Delano, issued in March of 1966 in the central California town of that name, defined the strike as *la causa* and as a Mexican American action for social justice. Delano served as the starting point for a march by hundreds of farm workers and supporters to the state capital in Sacramento. The plan, distributed to the public, based its philosophical roots in the universal struggle by workers of all races for economic and social justice. It proclaimed the protest march and UFW strike as the beginning of the Mexican American social movement for justice in the United States.

Over four million workers were employed by U.S. agriculture in low wage jobs at that time. The plan, distributed to the public, is considered a founding Chicano movement document that related to all Mexican American workers, not just farmworkers. It is important enough to be included here in its entirety:

The Plan of Delano

We the undersigned gathered in Pilgrimage to the capital of the State in Sacramento, in penance for all the failings of Farm Workers as free and sovereign men, do solemnly declare before the civilized world which judges our actions, and before the nation to which we belong, the propositions we have formulated to end the injustice that oppresses us.

We are conscious of the historical significance of our Pilgrimage. It is clearly evident that our path travels through a valley well known to all Mexican farm workers. We know all these towns of Delano, Fresno, Madera, Modesto, Stockton, and Sacramento, because along this very same road, in this very same valley, the Mexican race has sacrificed itself for the last hundred years. Our sweat and our blood have fallen on this land to make other men rich. Our wages and working conditions have been determined from above, because irresponsible legislators who could have helped us have supported the rancher's argument that the plight of the Farm Workers was a "special case." They saw the obvious effects of an unjust system, starvation wages, contractors, day hauls, forced migration, sickness, and subhuman conditions.

The farm worker has been abandoned to his own fate---without representation, without power---subject to the mercy and caprice of the rancher.

We are suffering. We have suffered unnumbered ills and crimes in the name of the Law of the land. Our men, women and children have suffered not only the basic brutality of stoop labor, and the most obvious injustices of the system; they have also suffered the desperation of knowing that the system caters to the greed of callous men and not to our needs.

Now we suffer for the purpose of ending the poverty, the misery, and the injustice, with the hope that our children will not be exploited as we have been. They have imposed hungers on us, and now we hunger for justice. We draw strength from the very despair in which we have been forced to life. WE SHALL ENDURE!

This Pilgrimage is a witness to the suffering we have seen for generations. The Penance we accept symbolizes the suffering we shall have in order to bring justice to these same towns, to this same valley. This is the beginning of a social movement in fact and not in pronouncements.

We seek our basic God-given rights as human beings. Because we have suffered---and we are not afraid to suffer---in order to survive, we are ready to give up everything, even our lives, in our fight for social justice. We shall do it without violence because that is our destiny.

To the ranchers and to all those who oppose us we say, in the words of Benito Juarez, "Respect for another's rights is the meaning of peace."

We seek the support of all political groups, and the protection of the government, which is also our government. But we are tired of words, of betrayals, of indifference. To the politicians we say that the years are gone when the farm worker said nothing and did nothing for himself. From this movement shall spring leaders who shall understand us, lead us, be faithful to us, and we shall elect them to represent us. We shall be heard!

We seek, and have, the support of the Church in what we do. At the head of the Pilgrimage we carry the Virgin of Guadalupe because she is ours, all ours, Patroness of the Mexican people. We also carry the Sacred Cross and the Star of David because we are not sectarians, and because we ask the help and prayers of all religions. All men are brothers, sons of the same God: that is why we say to all men of good will, in the words of Pope Leo XIII, "Everyone's first duty is to protect the workers from the greed of speculators who use human beings as instruments to provide themselves with money. It is neither just nor human to oppress with excessive work to the point where their minds become enfeebled and their bodies worn out." God shall not abandon us!

We shall unite. We have learned the meaning of unity. We know why these United States are just that---United. The strength of the poor is also in union. We know that the poverty of the Mexican or Filipino workers in California is the same as that of all farm workers across the country, the Negroes, the poor whites, the Puerto Ricans, Japanese and Arabians; in short all of the races that comprise the oppressed minorities of the United States. The majority of the people in our Pilgrimage are of Mexican descent, but the triumph of our race depends on a national association of farm workers. We must get together and bargain collectively. We must use only strength that we have, the force of our numbers; the ranchers are few, we are many. United we shall stand.

We shall pursue the Revolution we have proposed. We are sons of the Mexican Revolution, a revolution of the poor seeking bread and justice. Our revolution shall not be an armed one, but we want the order which now exists to be undone, and that a new social order replace it.

We are poor, we are humble, and our only choice is to Strike in those ranches where we are not treated with the respect we deserve as working men, where our rights as free and sovereign men are not recognized. We do not want the paternalism of the ranchers; we do not want the contractor; we do not want charity at the price of our dignity. We want to be equal with all the working men in the nation; we want a just wage, better working conditions, a decent future for all our children. To those who oppose us, be they ranchers, police, politicians, or speculators, we say that we are going to continue fighting until we die, or we win. We shall overcome!

Across the San Joaquin Valley, across California, the entire Southwest of the United States, wherever there are farm workers, our movement is spreading like flames across a dry plain. Our Pilgrimage is the match that will light our cause for all farm workers to see what is happening here, so that they may do as we have done.

The time has come for the liberation of the poor farm worker. History is on our side. May the strike go on! Viva la causa!

Activists in Los Angeles appreciated the goals of the Plan of Delano. It represented a collective consciousness of farm workers in the UFW about their own role in creating a historical social movement. They considered themselves as more than mere individuals who came together at this point in time in a mechanical response to hostile working conditions. Instead, they saw themselves forging a new movement characterized by sacrifice, suffering, joy, and victory. They pursued a collective strategy based on symbols of the Mexican flag and our Lady

of Guadalupe, along with an alliance of multiracial and interfaith supporters from all over the country.

Thus, UFW organizing efforts avoided exclusionary ethnic politics
that other Mexican American activist groups advocated. Instead, the
UFW involved thousands of people of diverse races, from different labor unions and community groups, and multi-faith religious activists
who represented the moral and economic power of churches. They all
took part in a movement led by Mexicans Americans.

The cry often heard at UFW events in Los Angeles was "Chicano
Power!" but the goal was economic justice for all workers and poor
people regardless of race.[1] The UFW newspaper *El Malcriado* (Bad
Manners) reached readers in Los Angeles and other U.S. communities
where Mexican Americans lived. This tiny publication helped build
unity against a powerful enemy: U.S. agribusiness. Winning the UFW
strike became the first goal and concrete first step towards organizing
the Chicano movement.[2] It also brought national attention to the UFW
and Chicanos on the march.

California Governor Ronald Reagan and U.S. Senator George
Murphy denounced the UFW and its growing movement as immoral
and dishonest, and characterized its supporters as blackmailers. They
rallied state power in defense of California agribusiness, intent on ruin-
ing the small farm workers union. The UFW strike, however, by now
had become *la causa* with wide support from urban Mexican Americans,
liberals, labor leaders and church groups. The UFW campaign faced
powerful enemies, but persisted in broadening and building a national
Mexican American Civil Rights Movement. Thus while some movement groups sometimes blamed powerful enemies for failures, the UFW
used powerful enemies to build a stronger movement.

National Attention

Although the UFW strike against California grape growers and boycott
of grapes posed no threat to the national economy, nor did it involve

25

street violence for national media attention, it soon forced the issue of social justice for farm workers to urban Mexican American workers and the national consciousness. Political groups and public officials across the nation chose sides between the UFW and California growers. The UFW strike and campaign gave substance, definition, and organization to the Mexican American *causa* or social movement. Cesar Chavez and Dolores Huerta kept the movement alive in travels throughout the nation and recruited allies through personal contact whenever possible. They created and sustained a national Mexican American passion for *la causa*.

Mexican American civic groups in Los Angeles embraced the UFW campaign and, as a result, pursued related employment goals for urban workers more aggressively. For example, on March 28, 1966, Los Angeles representatives of the League of Latin American Citizens (LULAC), the American GI Forum, Association of Mexican American Educators (AMAE), Mexican American Political Association (MAPA), and Council of Mexican American Affairs (CMAA) attended a conference sponsored by the federal Equal Employment Opportunities Commission (EEOC) in Albuquerque, New Mexico. Their purpose was to appeal for federal support of job training programs. But because only one of the five EEOC commissioners attended, the Los Angeles community representatives walked out to protest EEOC inattention. They continued to protest outside and sent a telegram of their complaint to President Johnson at the White House.[3]

The uproar created by the EEOC walkout assumed heroic dimensions among Mexican American activists. On April 28, 1966, one month later, activists from throughout the Southwest honored the walkout heroes at a banquet and ceremony at the Statler Hotel in downtown Los Angeles. They declared the day of the Albuquerque walkout, March 28, 1966, as the beginning of the Mexican American political "revolt," and called for more walkouts, marches, and mass protests for social justice across America.[4] Then in 1968, activists founded the National Council of La Raza in Washington, D.C. to support the Latino Civil Rights Movement nationally.

The rhetorical "revolt" became a metaphor for struggle. The appeal for militant action implied a clear need for organized, trained activists, an identifiable community base of support, and sufficient resources to create a revolt. But in spite of expressed unity, there was no shortcut to community organization and mobilization. Nonetheless, more activists, public events, militant rhetoric, and press conferences contributed to an upsurge of activism in Los Angeles.

Against the War in Vietnam

Mexican American opposition to the war in Vietnam became more prominent in East Los Angeles with the State Senate campaign by Democrat Richard Calderon, who ran on an anti-war platform in the election of June 1966. His aggressive anti-war campaign pulled Mexican American activists together against an incumbent Anglo State Assemblyman who was favored to win. Calderon lost by only 300 votes in a bitter contest. Voters at the same election also nominated conservative Republican Ronald Reagan for governor of California.

Calderon's loss was due in part to a new gerrymandered district with fewer Mexican American voters, an assumed Anglo voter backlash at increased Mexican American militancy, and to the campaign's blunt opposition to the war. In spite of the small margin of defeat, the Calderon campaign made opposition to the Vietnam War central to local Mexican American politics for the first time.

During the same spring, events in Denver affected the Mexican American movement in Los Angeles. In 1963, Corky Gonzales formed a group known as the Crusade For Justice, a militant civil rights Chicano organization. It helped popularize the term "Chicano" as a self-descriptive term for young native born Mexican Americans. The new name distinguished them as militants fighting for entitlement to all citizenship rights, including the right to full employment and a quality education. The Crusade For Justice advocated principles of cultural identity, nationalism, and struggle against an oppressive U.S. class system. It requested that the United Nations conduct a plebiscite in the U.S. Southwest to determine if Chicanos there preferred self-determination as a separate nation.[5] It advocated an aggressive Chicano "cultural nationalism" that influenced followers in Los Angeles.

During the 1966 "hot summer" of racial riots in major American cities, most Mexican American activists in Los Angeles continued to support the national anti-war movement. At that time, Rev. Martin Luther King Jr. denounced racism and the war after he discovered that Black troops were being killed on the battlefield in much higher rates than Anglo soldiers. Anti-war demonstrations across the nation became more frequent as the war continued with no end in sight.

Coalition Building

In the meantime, Mexican American activist groups in Los Angeles renewed attempts to form coalitions for political power. Coalitions, which became more common in the 1980's and 1990's, permitted activists and small groups to combine their limited resources for more power. As always, politicians knew which coalitions lacked an organized base of followers. In September of 1966, activists formed a successful coalition called the United Council of Community Organizations to select a consensus candidate for election to the Los Angeles Board of Education. In January 1967, at a coalition convention, over two hundred voting delegates from 36 community groups endorsed Julian Nava, a professor at California State University, Northridge, for election to the Los Angeles school board.[6]

The Nava campaign began with an initial budget of $750. He was an unknown Mexican American candidate from Northridge in the mostly white San Fernando Valley. He was up against an entrenched Anglo incumbent and had to reach over 1.4 million potential voters. But the Nava campaign, headed by Richard Calderon, involved diverse racial groups, labor unions, church groups, professional organizations, and liberal political groups across the giant school district.

Nava won the election.

The Nava victory opened greater opportunities for Mexican American educators in the Los Angeles public schools. It gave momentum to the drive for bilingual education programs and more Mexican American teachers became counselors, project administrators and school principals.

But in spite of major gains in school-based careers, the high dropout rate of Mexican American students continued to worsen. Mexican American teachers, like all others, were required to fit into an existing massive and inefficient public school bureaucracy, so they were unable to impact the high dropout rate of Mexican American students. This showed that progress made by Mexican American teachers needed to be supported by changes in school policy and administration to be effective.

True school reform had not been achieved. School parents remained powerless to realign the decision-making process for curriculum, personnel, and budget considerations at each school. Only independently organized school parents could have made changed the way schools operated -- and they did not exist. School staff "parent educators" assigned to educate parents on proper school support, were too entrenched in the school bureaucracy and unable to promote school reorganization. Nonetheless, the Nava victory contributed in a major way to the vision of a quality education for all children.

The alliance of Mexican American groups that met weekly to campaign for Nava's election to the school board evolved into a larger coalition. It adopted the name Congress of Mexican American Unity (CMAU) and by 1970 was reputed to have over 200 member organizations. (CMAU was led by Estevan Torres, who was later elected to Congress.) The coalition also attracted some of the more militant Chicano groups to its membership. Disputes over "politically correct" ideology turned group attention inward and hindered its potential to wield political power. As a result, CMAU eventually collapsed. During its existence, however, CMAU made major efforts to set up a permanent organization for community power – unfortunately, without lasting success.

Federal Advisory Committees

During this time, Chicano movement activists had not yet embraced the national feminist movement. Protest against racial discrimination continued without much reference to gender distinctions in local politics. But persistent demands for social justice for men and women in Los Angeles and across the Southwest moved the federal government to take notice of growing unrest. On June 9, 1967, the Johnson administration issued an executive order that established a cabinet level Inter-Agency Committee on Mexican American Affairs. Its announced role was to hear about problems in the Mexican American community, to assure a federal response, and to seek solutions.

Vicente T. Ximenes, who also served on the federal Equal Employment Opportunities Commission, headed the high-powered cabinet committee. It also included the Secretaries of Agriculture, Labor, Health, Education and Welfare, Housing and Urban Development, and the Director of the Office of Economic Opportunity. But even this concentration of government officials with a focus on the plight of the Mexican American people was insufficient to make a difference. Unfortunately, no community organization had the capacity to monitor the work of the cabinet committee, and for that reason it proved ineffective.

In spite of its good intentions, the cabinet committee turned out to be more public relations for the federal administration and less of a substantive effort to help the Mexican American people. Activists made serious attempts to provide information about local social conditions for consideration by the cabinet committee. But in truth, another government commission and study was a poor substitute for direct action to resolve community problems.

The federal cabinet committee held hearings in El Paso, Texas, on October 26-28, 1967 to hear invited testimony from representatives of Mexican American civic groups. Chicano activists from La Raza Unida, a new activist political group forming in Texas and California, argued strongly for a boycott of the hearings with and placed pickets outside the building.[7] But in spite of the picket line, other Mexican American representatives testified at the hearing. Differences in argument and tactics for direct action that emerged at the hearings contributed to the whole mosaic of building blocks in the evolving Chicano movement ideology and strategy for action.

The Los Angeles delegation testified about growing community frustration and anger over high unemployment and lack of job training programs. For example, Dionicio Morales,[8] executive director of the Mexican American Opportunities Foundation (MAOF), which was founded in 1963, warned of a grave possibility that Molotov cocktails might be used to attract national attention to the serious unemployment problem in Los Angeles. Ernesto Galarza from San Jose and Los Angeles Municipal Court Judge Philip Newman were among fifty representatives of Mexican American organizations who testified before the cabinet committee.

Outside the hearings, La Raza Unida members booed, hooted, and disrupted Texas Governor John Connally during his public remarks. Connally spoke at the ceremony calling for U.S. to return a disputed piece of land called "El Chamizal" to Mexico. Angry Chicano activists accused him of permitting the Texas Rangers to break farm worker strikes in the Rio Grande Valley. Even though the disruption outside the hearing received more attention than predictions inside of possible civil unrest in Los Angeles, media publicity of the disruption increased public awareness of a new Chicano militancy in the Southwest.

Vietnam War Casualties

Mexican American militancy against the war in Vietnam increased along with rising national public consciousness that this televised war was becoming larger, with increased U.S. casualties and no clear indication of military victory. Mexican American activists became more vocal in opposition to the war when, in June 1967, Congressman Henry B. Gonzalez[9] of San Antonio, Texas, reported in Congress that of 184 Texas soldiers who died in Vietnam, 60 had Spanish last names. Thus 33 percent of those killed had Spanish surnames, while that was true of only 14.8 percent of the Texas population. Gonzalez objected to the larger sacrifice of Spanish surnamed families in the cause of an unpopular war.

Three months later, the Mexican American Study Project at the University of California, Los Angeles (UCLA) issued a report that further documented a lopsided rate of Mexican American deaths in Vietnam. Based on 1960 census data, 19.9 percent of those killed in Vietnam were Mexican American soldiers compared to only 11.8 percent of their total population in California, Colorado, Arizona, New Mexico, and Texas. The higher death rate indicated that more Mexican American soldiers were assigned to high-risk front line military duty and that a disproportionate number of them fought and died on the battlefield.

The reports of unbalanced death rates by race in Vietnam provoked questions and much discussion among Mexican American activists. They expressed a deep concern over a high draft rate for Mexican American young men, who could not benefit from college deferment loopholes because they could neither afford to attend college nor could they afford lawyers to file lawsuits to avoid the draft. Wide dissemination of reports on the racist outcomes of the military draft generated high mistrust of the war and generated deeper resentment among Chicano youth.

In the meantime, established Mexican American groups like LULAC, the American GI Forum, the CSO, and MAPA adjusted slowly to deep currents of new politics that demanded faster social change. A younger generation of militant activists perceived established civic groups as a conservative force in politics and considered them as too closely allied with "establishment" politicians and special interests. Younger militant activists, mostly from the left, advocated a view of society as a struggle by a Chicano working class against a majority society fixated on accumulating wealth. They referred to older Mexican American civic groups as "assimilated" and -- worst of all -- "counter-revolutionary." The younger militants expressed more anger and began to call conservative groups *pendejos*, or stupid and unworthy of support.

Also in the fall of 1967, a group of writers at the University of California, Berkeley (UCB), led by Octavio Romano-V, published "El Grito, A Journal of Contemporary Mexican American Thought." It promoted retention of Mexican cultural identity as a primary responsibility of Chicano intellectuals and writers. At the same time, in Los Angeles on September 16, 1967, a group of Chicano activists published *La Raza*, a militant Chicano community newspaper. It circulated widely among movement groups and activists. A dedicated core of editors, writers, and photographers, headquartered in the basement of the Episcopal Church of the Epiphany in Lincoln Heights, provided left perspectives to a Chicano movement ideology then taking shape. Its articles hit hard at problems of an oppressed working class, including racist schools, police brutality, lack of political representation, and high unemployment. It urged Chicanos to fight capitalism at home instead of dying for imperialism in Vietnam.

La Raza also published poetry. In 1967, it presented "I Am Joaquin" by Corky Gonzales, leader of the Crusade For Justice in Denver. The poem became popular because of its interpretation of lost economic battles as victories of cultural survival, and called for a renewed spirit of revolution against capitalist forces. Its historical themes touched on *Gringo* (Anglos) oppression, cultural confusion, and survival of the Chicano people. Gonzales' poem was constantly quoted, play acted, and read in gatherings, meetings, and speeches. It became the best known poem of the Chicano movement.[10]

Articles in *La Raza* urged Chicano youth to refuse induction into the military service and, instead, to fight for justice against enemies in their own home town. Its articles aimed to agitate and to push Chicano activism to a more critical stance towards uncaring power elites in Los Angeles. It informed readers of movement events, like those surrounding Reies Lopez Tijerina, the evangelical preacher and leader of the Alianza Federal de Mercedes (Federal Alliance of Land Grants) in New Mexico.

Treaty Rights

Reies Lopez Tijerina charged in his "Plan de Ayala" that the U.S. government had violated the Treaty of Guadalupe Hidalgo when it allowed newly arrived Anglo settlers to take over Mexican land in the Southwest. He claimed title to 1,715 Spanish and Mexican land grants in California, Colorado, Arizona, New Mexico, Nevada, Texas, and Utah on behalf of 20,000 Alianza members. He wrote the Plan de Ayala to support this strategy to reclaim lost lands. He planed to have his followers trespass on a federal park in New Mexico to force the U.S. government to prosecute him. Once in court, he planed to challenge the legality of federal ownership of the land.[11]

In the spring of 1967, Tijerina's tactics escalated into a heated dispute with federal and local law enforcement officials. It led to Alianza members becoming involved in the dispute: they armed with guns to raid the Tierra Amarilla Courthouse. The raiding party released other Alianza members from jail and took over the courthouse for several hours. They held two hostages but later released them in the hills.[12] A combined force of 400 National Guardsmen, sheriffs, and police, with helicopter support and two tanks, searched the hills for Tijerina and his followers.

As Tijerina continued to elude capture, the news about Tierra Amarilla moved fast among activists in Los Angeles. Bits of news from radio and newspaper reports, excited telephone calls, and rumors circulated rapidly among movement activists across the city. The news conveyed from activist to activist was that a Mexican-style revolution had begun in the desert hills of New Mexico, and that U.S. military forces occupied small Mexican American communities in the search for Tijerina.

News of the search circulated rapidly, much like Paul Revere's ride warning that revolution was coming. Tijerina, eventually captured and released on bail, became a Chicano revolutionary hero to movement activists. Like a modern-day General Emiliano Zapata of the Mexican Revolution with a Plan de Ayala for redistribution of the land, Tijerina energized militant activism for return of the Chicano homeland to its rightful owners. He quickly moved to the forefront of la causa alongside Cesar Chavez and inspired the movement, although with different strategies.[13]

In Los Angeles, Chicano movement groups associated Tijerina's daring exploit with the anti-war and Civil Rights Movements. Militant Chicano youth, including college students who became more fluent in the use of left terminology, embraced Tijerina's anti-government armed action. They, in turn, passed their enthusiasm, zeal for revolution, and energy to other movement activists. They converted Tijerina into a symbol of Chicano armed resistance against repression. Some activists also cited his use of violence to achieve movement goals as an alternative to the pacifism and nonviolence of Cesar Chavez and the UFW.

Chavez and Tijerina shared common humble origins, without personal wealth or political influence, and with little formal education. They also shared a deep belief in God and Christian values of social justice.[14] But they differed on strategy and tactics. Chavez insisted on large numbers of organized participants and nonviolence to achieve goals, even in the face of violence by opponents. But Tijerina sparked a new consciousness for small-group direct action to promote justice, risking violence if necessary. He also embraced the long-term vision of possibly forming a new Chicano nation.

Most Chicano activists, however, discarded the notion of armed struggle as unnecessary, unrealistic, and impractical. Instead, movement groups proceeded to act more boldly in nonviolent protest against the war and for social justice at home.

Chapter 5

The Late Sixties

Brown Berets

By the late 1960's, Chicano activists became more restless as they asserted demands for jobs, a stop to police brutality, and an end to the war. At the same time, the national anti-war movement accelerated substantially with peaceful demonstrations, two mass protest marches in the nation's capital, militant civil disobedience, fights with police at demonstrations, and jailing of movement demonstrators across the country. Popular support for the war continued to lessen. In Vietnam, U.S. saturation bombing attacks continued on the North even as the South Vietnamese government began to fall apart.

In 1967, in Los Angeles, young Chicano men and women formed a small group called Young Citizens For Community Action. From that small nucleus, in 1968, a more militant organization emerged that became known as the Brown Berets, dedicated to "protect and serve" the Chicano community.[1] Brown Berets dressed in military style uniforms with their namesake brown berets and became visible at most Chicano protest demonstrations.

The Brown Berets, led by David Sanchez and Carlos Montes, complained of over-policing and police harassment of residents, and they held periodic protest demonstrations against police brutality. Like the Black Power movement, Brown Berets used blunt, fearless, angry words in public protest speeches against the war and the "pigs" (police) in the neighborhood. They quickly acquired a reputation for boldness in face-to-face confrontations with police on the streets.[2] I saw them march unafraid several times with picket signs, clenched fists, and loud yells demanding social justice.

The Brown Berets published their own newspaper, *La Causa*, that increased the flow of information about movement events and provided a political education for the whole community. It printed biting articles that denounced police harassment, ruling elites, and those they labeled Chicano "sellouts" or traitors to the movement. It called for "Chicano Power" and added fuel to anti-war, anti-gringo movement manifestos. It pounced on Anglo social institutions and "assimilated" Chicanos as the Chicano movement's most hated enemies.[3]

The Brown Berets called for an end to fights between barrio gangs. They repeatedly renewed calls for a united fight against a racist society. They criticized intellectuals and college students who studied the glorious Aztec culture of old Mexico, but who at the same time ignored hungry Chicano children in the barrio. Most of all, they denounced "Tio Tacos" and "vendidos" (sellouts) among anti-poverty workers, as well as professionals who remained silent about anti-Chicano racism in society.

The Brown Berets forged a self-image of Chicanos as a "brown people." This was an important distinction, since Chicanos ranged in skin color from dark brown to white, with eye colors of brown, black, grey, green, and blue, and hair colors of black, grey, white, blond, and red. But the image of brown skin, black hair, and dark eyes linked their identity with the Aztecs, creating a bridge between the original inhabitants of the Southwest -- burnt skinned people of the sun -- and revolutionary *soldados* (modern soldiers) in battle to reclaim their homeland. As modern Aztecs, they recreated a resistance to injustice. The Brown Berets had a major impact on the construction of movement demands. With fewer than a hundred active members in Los Angeles and limits as an organization, they nonetheless forced Los Angeles authorities to respond to them.[4] They helped create an issues agenda for the movement in East Los Angeles.

During their prominence, however, the Brown Berets demonstrated discipline, commitment, and a new militancy that helped gather large assemblies of people to propel the movement forward. They received a great deal of media coverage, including articles in national magazines like Newsweek.[5] They made an impact on the media because they focused on organizing protest events instead of operating with government funds. The Brown Berets also opened a medical Free Clinic in Boyle Heights, managed by Gloria Arrellanes, which served thousands of low-income community residents without charge. Even though the clinic was forced to close for lack of funds, the Brown Berets continued to promote Chicano pride and political awareness in all their activities. They rejected the image of a minority attached solely to physical labor in favor of a picture of a "brown people" of many skills and talents. They became the movement group most requested to lead or support protest demonstrations, mobilizations, and marches for justice and against the war.

The Brown Berets were most damaged when a Los Angeles police officer, posing as a militant Chicano, infiltrated the group. The infiltrator was suspected of encouraging unlawful actions so that Brown Berets could get arrested, and of informing the police of plans for action. Other movement groups expressed fear of infiltrators and police spies. In 1972, these infiltrations led David Sanchez, Brown Berets Prime Minister, to disband the Brown Berets but some activists claim it continues today.[6]

By 1968 the national anti-war movement was stronger than ever. The U.S. military admitted that the war in Vietnam was at a standstill and that heavy bombing and troop fighting would not end it. In California, even Governor Reagan, a staunch Republican, urged withdrawal of U.S. troops from Vietnam. In January, President Johnson declared that negotiations with North Vietnam would have to take place before cessation of U.S. bombing. At the same time, he requested additional funds to send more troops to Vietnam and denied a rumor that he had considered use of nuclear weapons to win the war.

Anti-war activists in Los Angeles received a big assist in February when Cesar Chavez began a 25-day fast to emphasize his commitment to nonviolence. He urged restraint, even in self-defense, to UFW strikers and supporters who faced violent attacks from growers in the fields. He also called for an end to the war in Vietnam and linked peace at home with peace in Vietnam.

Student Activism

At the same time, other Mexican American activists offered different guidelines for future action. The UCLA chapter of United Mexican American Students (UMAS) sponsored a conference on February 22, 1968, at the Westwood campus. Its goal was to identify collective goals for a united movement strategy. A large delegation of representatives from Los Angeles groups attended the conference, including members of the Brown Berets: UMAS chapters from Long Beach, Fresno, and Los Angeles: MAPA members from Los Angeles and Blyth: the Black Student Union and U.S. members from UCLA. The well-attended conference offered interpretations of social circumstances and directions for a rising Chicano movement.

An ad hoc committee invited representatives of movement groups, who spoke on a range of issues about the movement status. The speakers included University professor Ralph Guzman, Crusade for Justice Corky Gonzales, Federal Alliance of Land Grants leader Reies Lopez Tijerina, UFW Teatro Campesino leader Luis Valdez, and others. They spoke on the plight of immigrant workers, persistent poverty, police brutality, inferior education, retention of the Spanish language and Mexican culture, and opposition to the war. The master of ceremonies was Eliezer Risco, co-editor with Joe Razo of La Raza newspaper. The audience clapped, cheered and yelled "Viva La Raza!" (Long live the race!) and "Viva la Revolucion!" Speakers reiterated anger at familiar problems and pointed to the road towards social justice.

More than any other speaker, Reies Lopez Tijerina of New Mexico electrified an already enthusiastic audience. He symbolized armed resistance against repression in society. Risco introduced Tijerina as the "Citizen Number One of *La Raza Nueva*," and the young activist audience yelled, cheered and let him know they backed his aggressive militant posture.

Tijerina spiced his remarks with colorful language to describe the enemy U.S. government and Anglo society.[7] He used enemy metaphors like "criminals," "beasts," and "blue-eyed buffalos." His words turned the dominant Anglo society into "pirates," "blue-eyed cats" and "stupid giants." When he predicted that the United States would lose the war in Vietnam, the audience rose to its feet with enthusiastic, sustained applause. He said the Vietnamese would win because they were fighting a foreign invader in their own homeland. He also said that Chicanos would some day walk on their own homeland in peace and justice in a new social order. He shouted over the noisy applause that the Chicano revolution had already begun. He called for a heritage of valor for future Chicano generations, not pink cards for powdered milk on welfare lines -- what he labeled "a heritage of animals, not of a courageous people."

Tijerina's speech had a soul-stirring effect on the activist student audience. Listeners rose to applaud with cheers, foot stomping, and hand clapping. He touched raw nerves with every metaphor and stinging attack against an enemy majority society. His rhetorical "kill" of the enemy inspired high hopes for success of a revolutionary Chicano movement. The impassioned rhetoric touched the awareness, analysis, and feelings that came from the heart of a people determined to undo social injustice.

Ten years later, after serving two years in a federal prison for the jail house raid, Tijerina changed tactics. By 1973, he advocated a multiracial brotherhood for which Chicano movement activists then criticized him.[8] Nonetheless, Tijerina's speech at the UCLA conference was an uplifting emotional experience that agitated student listeners.

Educational Issues Coordinating Committee

The high school student walkouts and their demands for better schools remained unmet. But by their status, student activists were transitory and unable to sustain the walkouts or to negotiate a settlement with school officials. Most students returned to class after a week, but a core of holdouts announced that the Educational Issues Coordinating Committee (EICC), which evolved out of the emergency committee, would henceforth present student demands to school officials. EICC consisted at first of a loosely structured gathering of school parents, students, labor and community activists, local residents, and later, of Mexican American professionals. Sal Castro, a teacher at Lincoln High School in Lincoln Heights, emerged as the leader of students and activists who organized the student strike. His appeal to students was "*No sean mensos* (Don't be fools), go to college and graduate." As an activist teacher, he demonstrated a challenging role for other Chicano teachers. Rev. Vahac Mardirosian, director of a Protestant Hispanic outreach project in East Los Angeles, served as EICC chairman and made presentations at school board meetings.

Much larger political developments in America were then taking place, including the assassination of Rev. Martin Luther King in April in Memphis, followed by the June assassination of U.S. Senator and presidential candidate Robert Kennedy in Los Angeles. These two assassinations, as well as the riots in U.S. cities after the death of Rev. King, renewed dedication in the national Civil Rights Movement for jobs, good schools, and peace in America. These events also formed part of the political context for the ensuing Chicano movement in Los Angeles.

On May 30, 1968, the weekend before the primary election, the Los Angeles County Grand Jury secretly indicted 13 Chicano activists for conspiracy to disrupt the public schools in the March high school walkouts. The County Sheriff's department, the city police department, and the District Attorney's Office conducted a 12-week undercover investigation that led to this secret indictment.[9]

The grand jury met for three days and heard testimony from more than 50 witnesses. The "evidence" presented included testimony that the Brown Berets, who supported the student strike, also supported other movement groups, such as the Students for a Democratic Society (SDS) and the Alianza movement of Reies Lopez Tijerina in New Mexico. The grand jury charged that the student strike was not spontaneous, but the result of a conspiracy by non-students to disrupt the educational process at Garfield, Roosevelt, Lincoln, and Belmont high schools.

Most indicted activists were arrested and were in jail the following day. Over 150 members of various Chicano movement groups responded immediately with three days of protest demonstrations in front of the downtown police headquarters. They denounced the arrests and set up a picket line with chants and signs that supported the jailed activists. The American Civil Liberties Union (ACLU) assailed the grand jury charges as clumsy and unwarranted by the evidence. It also condemned the $10,000 bail set by the court for each defendant as excessive, punitive, and designed to suppress freedom of speech and association in the Chicano community. To put it in context, this bail was ten times higher than the usual amount set for a charge of burglary and twice the usual amount for a charge of assault with a deadly weapon.[10]

John Greenlee, President of Cal State L.A., was among the first civic leaders to object to the overzealous manner in which the arrests were carried out. According to the Los Angeles Times, he said that the manner of applying justice in this case exposed the system of justice to question by the entire community.[11] He cited the early morning arrests, the secrecy of the grand jury proceedings and indictments, and the excessive bail as reprehensible acts. As a member of the faculty at Cal State L.A., I felt proud of how our university president responded.

District Attorney Evelle J. Younger charged those arrested with conspiracy to disturb the peace. The conspiracy charge turned an individual act of disturbing the peace, a misdemeanor, into a felony. The use of the conspiracy theory marked the start of a new legal weapon to be used against militant activists involved in direct social protest.

Activists against the arrests picketed in front of the Hall of Justice. Inside, on June 3, 1968, the Superior Court reduced bail for the defendants, who included activists, college instructors, and high school teacher Sal Castro. Others indicted were not yet arrested, but those in jail posted bail for release.[12]

Tough law and order candidates won the 1968 primary election, including District Attorney Younger and a slate of school board candidates who campaigned against EICC protest tactics. The new school board members assumed majority control of the schools for years to come and kept their pledge to oppose militant Chicano activists on public school issues. This conservative takeover of the schools was an unanticipated consequence of the series of events traceable to the Chicano student walkouts.

Another unanticipated consequence was a failed attempt by Governor Ronald Reagan to set up a liaison with Mexican American activists in East Los Angeles. The governor announced the selection of Ralph Morales, a policeman from Los Angeles, to work as liaison with the local Mexican American community.[13] Morales, however, vanished from public view after the grand jury indictments. His disappearance followed by one day the public announcement of his appointment. He would have been regarded as a known infiltrator for law enforcement.

Advancements of the national anti-war movement and falling popularity of President Lyndon Johnson combined to foster more intense social protest in Los Angeles. By now, at the national level, President Johnson announced a partial stop to the bombing of North Vietnam, and in a clear concession to the national anti-war movement, he declared that he would not be a candidate for reelection. By this move, he said he hoped to heal divisiveness in the country over the war. The anti-war movement, however, continued to gain followers across the nation and in Los Angeles.

In Los Angeles, EICC and the Congress of Mexican American Unity (CMAU) developed a defense of the indicted Chicano activists, who were facing possible prison terms for the school walkouts. EICC and CMAU raised legal defense funds and directed community pressure against the District Attorney. Eventually, the legal defense succeeded in getting all the charges dropped. Attorney Oscar Acosta announced at an anti-police demonstration on August 6, 1970, that the successful defense set a legal precedent for Los Angeles: that Chicanos, students or non-students, had a right to organize students on a school campus, and that violence, if it occurred during a campus demonstration, cannot be necessarily inferred as coming from the organizers of a campus demonstration.[14]

In the meantime, EICC held a series of mass protest demonstrations at the main offices of the board of education to demand reassignment of Lincoln High School teacher Sal Castro, one of the defendants, from routine clerical work at school district headquarters back to his teaching duties at Lincoln High School. This punitive move was intended to remove Castro from contact with students who respected and trusted him. The demonstrations led to further polarization and neither side conceded nor negotiated a settlement, although the school district later reassigned Castro from clerical work to a teaching position at neighboring Belmont High School.[15] He became a time-honored example for teachers and students that Mexican Americans are capable of graduation from high school and college.

Mexican American Education Commission

The intransigency of the schools provoked EICC to mount almost weekly mass protest demonstrations over a two-year period. Many community activists were introduced to social protest activities at those demonstrations. On July 18, 1968, EICC requested that it be recognized as an official independent commission of the school board, charged with investigating issues raised by the students or teachers. The school board instead accepted the administration's rebuttal to student demands, but it agreed with the need for Spanish speaking school personnel and to a reduction in class size. However, EICC objected to its lack of participation in school decisions and again requested that it be given legal status as an independent commission of the school board. Protests, activities, and demonstrations continued.[16]

While focused mostly on local issues, Chicano activists in Los Angeles saw televised riots of thousands of anti-war demonstrators at the 1968 Democratic National Convention in Chicago that nominated Vice President Hubert Humphrey for President. In the meantime, EICC protest demonstrations increased in frequency with greater numbers of protestors, including an October sit-in at the offices of the Board of Education that lasted six days and nights. Ralph Guzman, a professor at Cal State L.A., identified the dramatic sit-in for better schools as the first appearance of "Brown Power" in Los Angeles.[17] It forced many people to reexamine their assumptions about Mexican American politics as passive to injustice. It changed the political perception that Mexican Americans were submissive people to an appreciation of their growing power.

When Richard Nixon defeated Humphrey to win the 1968 presidential election, he promised to represent what he called the "silent majority" in America. He said it opposed street protest demonstrations and favored conventional politics to resolve political differences.

At the same time in Los Angeles, EICC faced hard times. Its membership dwindled due to the attraction of other movement groups and events. There were many new small groups with new leaders as partners in the overall action for justice. Over time, only a residue core group of committed activists remained involved.

The remaining EICC activists pursued their own talks with the school board to request official standing in February 1969. The school board gave new attention to the EICC request and activists thought it would happen. Then in April of that year, the Los Angeles Board of Education created the Mexican American Education Commission

(MAEC), with authority to hire a director and secretary. A negotiated MAEC membership included parents, teachers, professors, students, and professionals. This met EICC expectations of an important step towards better schools. EICC chairman Rev. Mardirosian subsequently formed and headed the Hispanic Urban Center in Boyle Heights. The center was separate from EICC and militant activists. It operated in part under contract with the public schools to train teachers and staff to teach Mexican American students. The public schools finally recognized that course content on Mexican American culture and history in the public school benefited the education of Mexican American students and others.

However, street protests for better schools continued. On March 6, 1970, a strike by over 250 students and adults demanded better instruction at Roosevelt High School in Boyle Heights. They commemorated the second anniversary of the 1968 student walkouts with a new demand for quality schools. They protested a high dropout rate, racist IQ testing, and demanded courses in Chicano history and literature. The police arrested several students during this protest. The following day, more than 200 students picketed in front of the Hollenbeck police station in Boyle Heights to denounce police brutality against student protestors. Students carried out another protest demonstration on March 9 against inferior education at the school.

Continuing protests over inferior schools led to the creation of the Mexican American Education Commission (MAEC), an important victory for EICC. The commission, led by Raul Arreola, added a new tactic to the quest for better schools by generating pressure to change the schools from the inside. In reality, however, MAEC had to overcome stiff resistance from school administrators to improve school quality and involvement of parents in the schools.

Even so, MAEC achieved notable success. It defended Mexican American teachers and students against racist school practices, and it developed and monitored a grievance procedure to handle student and parent complaints. It also replaced the usual report card with parent-teacher conversations and progress reports, an innovation later adopted throughout the school district.

In 1973, MAEC reported some progress toward better schools.[18] It defended Mexican American teachers from unfair teacher evaluations, assisted parents in pursuing complaints against the schools, and recommended more relevant course content. But even with good intentions, MAEC functioned more in a liaison role between school officials and school parents. Over time, it operated like part of the school bureaucracy, with limited capacity to organize school families so they could obtain meaningful power.

EICC met weekly in large gatherings. It attracted a fluctuating attendance of activists who debated issues such as deficient education and dropout rates, tactics, parliamentary motions, and "correct" ideology. Those present at a particular meeting, not always the same individuals, voted and approved decisions for collective action. As authors Joan Moore and Armida Martinez indicate, political posturing, factional power plays for control, and spirited debates on "correct" political ideology eventually diminished participation of the working poor.[19]

As a result, EICC became an organization of more middle class activists and professionals. Yet it kept the Chicano movement fired up with mass social protests. And solidified the movement's "militant" image. But even after EICC led the courageous hard fight, with demonstrations, mass protests, jailing's, defense committees, sit-ins, and packed school board meetings, the Los Angeles public schools remained inferior. Mexican American children still attended schools that produced unacceptable dropout rates and low levels of achievement in basic skills, where parents remained without true power to participate in school decisions.

For its part, EICC was unable to organize sufficient community support to implement significant change in the schools. University of California History professor Carlos Munoz Jr. points out that EICC went into action without first involving a critical mass of the Mexican American people to create more viable support.[20]

48

Thus, EICC eventually became one of those transitory groups that are typical in social movements. In reality, its major accomplishment was that it trained activists. It introduced hundreds of Chicano activists to their first experiences in social protest as participants in the national Civil Rights Movement.

During and after the walkouts, groups like EICC, MAEC and others generated unprecedented energy in local politics. Activists became more noticeable at public events and demonstrations. In the summer of 1968, activists in El Sereno published *Con Safos*, a quarterly magazine on racism, class exploitation, unequal education, police brutality, poetry, essays, and art. Its core group leaders included Arturo Flores, Gil Gonzales, Rodolfo Salinas, and Francisco Sifuentes. The magazine title was Chicano --slang for "back to you," a fight-back gesture.

Chicano Studies Department

News of the high school student walkout and EICC battles with the school board reached college campuses. Chicano student activists demanded a new academic department that focused on the history, literature, and contributions of Mexican Americans to U.S. history. Faculty and administration supported student demands, and at Cal State LA, a new academic department was formed: the Department of Mexican American Studies. By the end of 1968, chapters of United Mexican American Students (UMAS) had formed on other area colleges. UMAS later became Movimiento Estudiantil Chicano de Aztlan (MECHA) and promoted a student identity as militant "Chicanos" in contrast to more assimilated and conservative "Mexican Americans." This development reminded me that when I graduated from the same campus in 1957, I learned about racism against Blacks and the Civil Rights Movement, but heard almost nothing about anti-Mexican racism and the maltreatment of immigrant families.

The college student movement had its own social process of beginning, decline, and renewal.[21] The student movement overcame factions, conflicts, and disputes between groups to survive. It mobilized support for the larger off-campus movement and fought on campus for financial aid, relevant programs and courses, and for open admissions. Activist students supported the establishment of student service programs, such as the Educational Opportunities Program (EOP), Educational Participation In Communities (EPIC), and the Pat Brown Institute of Public Affairs. Activist Chicano college students accentuated their new self-identity at campus gatherings with shouts of "Chicano Power!" and "*Viva La Raza.*" Like the emerging off-campus movement, many students espoused variations of Marxism and Chicano nationalism in the college student movement.[22]

Beginning in 1968, students in my classes often prompted classroom discussion of implications of the Chicano high school student walk-out. At the same time, the first in the nation Department of Mexican American Studies was formed with support from off-campus activists.[23] At the urging of more militant activist students, the name of the department was later changed to Department of Chicano Studies. Student activists from some campuses met in Santa Barbara and proposed guidelines for development of Chicano Studies departments statewide based on cultural identity and working class struggles.

Cal State LA, like the high schools, responded to the challenge of creating a program to reflect the culture and aspirations of Mexican American students. As stated earlier, I served as Director of Project Head Start in Lincoln Heights when in 1968, I was recruited by Professor Robert Kully, my college debate coach, to teach a course in the Speech Department at my alma mater, Cal State LA. About the same time, I accepted an invitation by students and faculty to serve as a founding member of the new Mexican American Studies department, then chaired by high school teacher, Rudy Holquin.

But first I was interviewed for the faculty position by a *Mesa Directiva* (board of directors), an unofficial, loosely structured campus Chicano activist group, with an understanding that whoever showed up could vote. *La Mesa Directiva* met in the basement of the library as an advisory group with a mixture of a small number of students, faculty, and movement activists, including the Brown Berets. It was an exciting time for all of us. I was asked about my support for the Chicano movement. I told of my experience prior to Head Start when I served as Consultant to the Committee on State Personnel and Military Affairs of the California State Assembly, and that as a result I was familiar with state politics and Mexican American issues. I also told of my experience as recipient of a Coro Foundation Fellowship In Public Affairs in San Francisco. I expressed my support for efforts to begin a new academic department. I was pleased that the Mesa Directiva recommended approval of my teaching appointment.

The Chicano movement was in full steam and we were part of it. Student shouts of "Chicano Power!" would erupt almost everywhere on campus. *La Mesa Directiva* was symbolic of community support of the new academic department and my position on it. Other full-time and part-time faculty who contributed to development of the department included Francisco Balderrama, Roberto Cantu, Alfred Carmona, Bert Corona, Manuel DeOrtega, Miguel Dominquez, Jorge Illueca, David Lopez-Lee, Hector Soto-Perez, Rudy Quinones, Richard Santillan, and Carlos Vasquez.

Our faculty and students joined hundreds of community activists in off-campus picketing, protest demonstrations, and marches that characterized those times. Some of my students met Cesar Chavez while we marched on the United Farm Workers picket line in front of the Safeway Market in Lincoln Heights to oppose California grape growers. The students were impressed with Chavez, who seemed humble and intensely committed to the UFW. Activist Chicano lawyer Oscar Acosta likewise impressed my students when he spoke to my class about the fight for social justice so much that they gave him a standing ovation.

Appreciation and support on campus were evident for the Chicano struggle for social justice. Students from all disciplines openly opposed the war and police abuse, and defended immigrant workers and their families. They took to picket lines to support labor unions for fair treatment on the job. They joined in civil disobedience and demonstrations

51

of the Educational Issues Coordinating Committee (EICC) to follow up on the demands of the high school walkouts. They contributed to the image of the Department of Chicano Studies as an academic department with an activist student component.

The new department began with mostly part-time faculty. Few of us had advanced degrees and none of us had prior experience in operating a university academic department. But we had the support of the administration, a shared vision, and a common understanding that we were embarking on something brand new in higher education, something revolutionary. I served as Department Chair for three years. With broad community support, we began to build a more relevant and academic study of the Chicano experience and contributions to U.S. society.

We also insisted on making the university more accessible to Chicano students. We aimed to attract a greater number of Chicano students for all college majors across the curriculum in the natural and social sciences, humanities, and health sciences. At the same time, all students would have an option to include courses that emphasized the Chicano contributions to American history, Mexican culture and history, retention of the Spanish language, and a commitment to principles of democracy in U.S. society.

We were the first university in the country to offer courses on Mexican folk dances. Emilio Pulido taught the courses that attracted many high school dancers to enroll at our campus. We also offered courses in mariachi music and art as part of cultural identity. Some of our students were among the first street mural artists in Los Angeles. Untouched walls in our neighborhoods and on campus became Chicano murals that kept the spirit of the Chicano movement alive.

We also developed our own publications. Faculty members David Lopez Lee published the Journal of Cultural Studies, and in 1976, Roberto Cantu organized the department Publications Center. He edited two journals, *Campo Libre* in the social sciences and *Escolios* in language and literature. Cantu also organized international conferences on campus focused on Chicano literature and history, which included writers and scholars invited from nations in Europe, Africa,

Asia, and South America. The department has acquired an international reputation for the academic study of Chicano history and literature. As a result, the university faculty honored both Francisco Balderrama and Roberto Cantu with Outstanding Professor Awards.

My first initiative in the department was to eliminate the university requirement that our majors complete an "ancillary major" which required an additional major. Mexican American Studies was not yet considered a stand alone true major. With faculty approval, I wrote a proposal for a freestanding major in Mexican American Studies that the University approved in 1971. Later, I wrote a proposal for a Master of Arts Degree in Mexican American Studies that was approved in 1977. I also proposed an option within our major for a multiple subjects credential for elementary school teachers and an option for a single subject credential for high school teachers. Both teacher education options were approved, but later taken over by the Education Department.

The new degree majors included contributions and support from department faculty with different academic backgrounds. Our academic programs identified academic stereotypes of Chicanos as a subordinate group of people accustomed to life in the margins of society, and instead presented contributions of Mexican Americans in the fields of literature, history, and contemporary affairs.

Our faculty and students wrote and spoke in English and Spanish. They told stories of themselves, their immigrant families, and community, and expressed knowledge of important historical and cultural contributions to U.S. democracy. New academic research literature began to take shape. It came from papers presented at conferences, chapters in anthologies, and books devoted to documentation of the Chicano experience. The faculty and students encouraged waves of more Chicano students to attend the university regardless of field of study. As the department undergraduate advisor, I recognized that our graduates would sustain a community surge of energy to fight poverty and injustice in our own neighborhoods. At the national level, there now exists a National Association of Chicana Chicano Studies (NACCS) to promote Chicano Studies.

Chapter 6

Aztlan

Chicano Homeland

At the end of the Sixties, national turmoil and unrest increased in opposition to the war in Vietnam. More direct violent confrontations occurred between civil rights activists -- including the Black Panthers -- and government authorities. Mexican American groups across the country applied constant pressure on government officials for full civil rights.

A response came from President Johnson in one of his last presidential appointments when, in November 1968, he appointed Hector P. Garcia of Texas, founder of the American GI Forum, to the U.S. Commission on Civil Rights. The Commission held hearings in San Antonio on December 9 to 14, 1968, to review civil rights problems in the Southwest. Rev. John B. Luce, pastor of Epiphany Church in Lincoln Heights, and Armando Morales, a psychiatric social worker, made a joint presentation on behalf of the Community Service Organization (CSO), League of United Latin American Citizens (LULAC), Association of Mexican American Educators (AMAE), American GI Forum, Mexican American Political Association (MAPA), and the Council of Mexican American Affairs (CMAA).[1]

Presenters objected to police repression in Los Angeles and pointed to worsening tension between Mexican American activists and Los Angeles police and sheriff's departments. They predicted serious direct confrontations

54

unless the federal government intervened to protect the community from the police. Eventually, federal grants were awarded to a few Mexican American civic groups, like the Mexican American Opportunities Foundation (MAOF), the Council of Mexican American Affairs (CMAA), the League of Latin American Citizens (LULAC), and the American GI Forum for job training programs and Head Start projects. These organizations were more middle class and not strictly protest groups. Overall, the Commission was more helpful with documented reports about racist practices in society than in its defense of the civil rights of minorities.

Social circumstances continued to deteriorate for the masses of Mexican Americans in Los Angeles. Families in East Los Angeles lacked the power to participate fully in democracy or to change things in a scale large enough to reduce poverty. This lack of power occurred in spite of political appointments of community activists to advisory boards, special committees, and commissions. Such appointments to government advisory commissions seemed to be an improvement, but they had more publicity value for politicians and for individual appointees than for increasing true community-based political power. That's because testimony given to advisory commissions led to publicity, not to community power. Access to advisory boards, after all, differs from the true exercise of power. Professional appointees to advisory commissions were more concerned with issues of the middle class, not of the working poor.[2]

In the meantime, young Chicano activists and college and high school students in Los Angeles continued to seek movement unity. In March, 1969, some of them attended a conference in Denver led by Corky Gonzales and his Crusade For Justice. The goal was to set a common agenda. They met with over 1,000 students and activists from other states and adopted resolutions that collectively formed *El Plan Espiritual de Aztlan.*[3]

The Plan, as it came to be known, was adopted at a time in world history when the concept of a nation still correlated with ethnic identity, unlike today when nations include people from diverse cultures and languages. Nationalism's appeal to ethnicity nonetheless made it useful to provide identity to Chicanos. The Plan for Chicano Nationalism was recited, copied, and republished throughout the Southwest. It set forth a poetic and ideological identification of the U.S. Southwest as the original homeland of all Chicanos. It issued a clarion call for return of the Chicano homeland and Chicano nationalism. Its introduction reads as follows:

El Plan Espiritual de Aztlan

"In the spirit of a new people that is conscious not only of its proud historical heritage but also of the brutal "gringo" invasion of our territories, we, the Chicano inhabitants and civilizers of the northern land of Aztlan from whence came our forefathers, reclaiming the land of their birth and consecrating the determination of our people of the sun, declare that the call of our blood is our power, our responsibility, and our inevitable destiny

We are free and sovereign to determine those tasks which are justly called for by our house, our land, the sweat of our brows, and by our hearts. Aztlan belongs to those who plant the seeds, water the fields, and gather the crops and not to the foreign Europeans. We do not recognize capricious frontiers on the bronze continents.

Brotherhood unites us, and love for our brothers makes us a people whose time has come and who struggle against the foreigner "gabacho" who exploits our riches and destroys our culture. With our heats in our hands and our hands in the soil, we declare the independence of our mestizo nation. We are a bronze people with a bronze culture. Before the world, before all of North America, before all our brothers in the bronze continent, we are a nation, we are a union of free pueblos, we are Aztlan."

The Plan de Aztlan became an important social document for the Chicano movement. Rudolfo A. Anaya, recognized as a founder of

Chicano literature, referred to it as part of a "naming ceremony" vital to the movement for history, identity, and purpose.[4] It pledged Chicanos to struggle for restoration and political control of Aztlan, the mythical ancestral Aztec homeland acquired from Mexico under terms of the Treaty of Guadalupe Hidalgo at the end of the U.S. invasion of Mexico. Movement activists fervently espoused its mythical and historical dimensions as an ideological premise for struggle in modern society.[5]

Corky Gonzales carried the message of the *Plan de Aztlan* from Denver to Los Angeles at a conference sponsored by UMAS on April 16, 1969 at Claremont College. According to the Los Angeles Times, over 700 conferees discussed the roles of United Mexican American Students (UMAS), American GI Forum, Mexican American Political Association (MAPA), League of Latin American Citizens (LULAC), Community Service Organization (CSO), Association of Mexican American Educators (AMAE), and the Brown Berets.[6] They searched for common bonds to unify the Chicano movement. Gonzales attacked racist public schools and urged Chicano nationalism as the primary defense against all forms of U.S. racism.[7] The call for unity took on a life of its own as a major point in movement discourse, while the search continued for a concrete plan on how to do it.

Courtroom Battles

In the meantime, Mexican American activists applied administrative and legal pressure against English-only tests used to measure the "intelligence" of Spanish speaking students. The predictable result of those tests was a high rate of Mexican American pupils classified as "educable mentally retarded." When the same students were administered the same test in Spanish, they scored significantly higher.[8] When the California state Department of Education made this "discovery," it stopped this most blatantly inappropriate and racist testing.[9] The judgment of school officials began to change slowly to recognize the language and cultural differences of Mexican American students.

At the same time, the California State Department of Education issued a revealing report on the status of more than 600,000 Mexican American students in the California public schools.[10] This shocking report stated that 50 percent would not complete the 8th grade and 73 percent would not finish high school. This report fueled ongoing complaints by activists about the low quality of education statewide for Mexican American students.[11]

A small group of Chicano movement activists took their fight for better schools directly to Governor Ronald Reagan. They confronted him at the April 24, 1969 *Nuevas Vistas* (New Visions) State Department of Education conference on Mexican American students, held at the Biltmore Hotel in downtown Los Angeles. Governor Reagan addressed a large audience of educators, including Mexican American teachers and school administrators, on the necessity of educating students from bilingual homes to compete in society.[12]

As he spoke of two million Californians of Mexican descent who needed bilingual education, more than twenty Chicano militant demonstrators -- mostly Brown Berets -- yelled, chanted, and marched around the room to disrupt his speech. A fire broke out in the hotel and Governor Reagan was unable to continue with his prepared remarks. Police officers arrested some of the demonstrators and took them to jail. Afterwards, a grand jury charged them with conspiracy, arson, burglary, burning personal property, and malicious destruction of electrical wires.[13]

This type of direct confrontation and interference by small movement groups became a common protest tactic over the next few years. They frustrated "enemy" speakers, disrupted activities, gave high visibility to "revolutionary" struggle, and helped consolidate an aggressive pursuit of social justice. These sporadic, dramatic, and forceful tactics continued to motivate activists. As a result, the media portrayed the larger movement in radical terms.

Civil rights lawyers, including Oscar Z. Acosta from the Mexican American Legal Defense and Education Fund (MALDEF), got involved in the case and won dismissal of the charges against the Biltmore Hotel demonstrators. Acosta said that the political issue was survival of the Chicano movement itself against a deliberate attempt to destroy it.[14] He blamed the hotel fires on an undercover Los Angeles police officer who posed as a Brown Beret. When Acosta probed into the issue of racial discrimination in the selection of the grand jury itself, the trial turned into a heated personal dispute with Superior Court Judge Arthur Alarcon, who jailed Acosta for contempt of court.[15]

Acosta, however, forced the court to admit that Mexican Americans were a separate and distinct class of people who could not be lumped together with Caucasians for constitutional compliance for a jury of peers.[16] This decision about service on juries had ongoing impact, as it forced the courts to render more attention to the racial and ethnic composition of future grand juries in Los Angeles.

Judges themselves were not above criticism. On September 2, 1969, while hearing a case, San Jose Superior Court Judge Gerald S. Chargin referred to the Mexican American people as "animals." He said that maybe Hitler was right that animals in society should be destroyed.[17] The Community Service Organization (CSO) chapter in San Jose and the California Rural Legal Assistance Office alerted Chicano activists across the state about Judge Chargin's racist and in-flammatory remarks. Universal demands for his disqualification as a judge were swift and widespread,[18] including a Los Angles Times editorial that demanded his removal from the bench for hostile and bigoted courtroom remarks.[19]

A coalition of Mexican American activists and other civil rights groups met with court officials in San Jose, who responded that noth-ing could be done. Judge Chargin said in his own defense that court comments were harsh in some cases to lecture youthful defendants. But to Chicano activists in Los Angeles, this case illustrated anti-Mexican racism inside the California judicial system. Black activist groups and elected officials also denounced racism in the courts. This controversy increased tension in race relations in Los Angeles and provoked Chicano movement groups into more activity.

More Advisory Boards

Government moves to appoint advisory boards became a tactic to ultimately weaken the movement. This tactic worked among the middle-
class organizations. In the meantime, President Nixon activated the role
of the federal government regarding problems affecting the Mexican
American people.[20] Over the objections of Mexican American activists in the Republican Party, in April of 1969, the President appointed Los Angeles attorney Martin Castillo to head a new Inter-Agency
Committee on Mexican American Affairs.[21] This new federal committee had its own 27-member staff and could call on specialists from other
branches of the federal government for special assignments. Its mission was to gather information on the plight of the Mexican American
people and to propose federal action for solutions.[22]

The committee later changed its name to the Cabinet Committee
On Opportunity For The Spanish-Speaking in order to include Puerto
Rican and Cuban American groups. It reiterated its promise to examine
school dropout rates for Mexican Americans and Puerto Ricans, and to
develop policy options to deal with poverty in Hispanic areas. Castillo
saw the work of the cabinet committee as part of the Mexican American
movement for social justice.[23] He blamed ideological and personality
"conflict among ourselves" for the lack of coordination or direction for
the entire Mexican American movement.

The Mexican American Political Association (MAPA) objected to a
statement by President Nixon that more Mexican Americans served in
his administration than any other. MAPA rejected the implication that
more qualified candidates could not be found to serve in government.[24]
Instead of weaving together a network of civic groups for inclusion, the
cabinet committee conducted surveys, disseminated information, and
sponsored conferences to present and hear reports.

The cabinet committee also noted the lack of Hispanic American-
owned businesses. In 1973, Henry M. Ramirez, the new cabinet
committee chairman, identified a litany of continuing despair among

Spanish-speaking people.[25]   But his main concern was to continue congressional funding for the cabinet committee. In the meantime, Mexican American and other Hispanic civic groups criticized the cabinet committee staff for campaigning to reelect President Richard Nixon in 1974 instead of helping the Spanish-speaking people.

In spite of support from groups like the American GI Forum, Operation SER-Jobs For Progress, and several Miami-based Cuban American groups, overall public support fell apart for the Cabinet Committee On Opportunities for Spanish-Speaking People.[26]   Henry Ramirez, its chairman, resigned. After the Watergate scandal forced President Nixon to resign, President Gerald Ford appointed Fernando E.C. de Baca, a Texas Republican, as a special presidential assistant with the same responsibilities previously assigned to the entire cabinet committee.[27]   His appointment did not improve movement relations with the White House.

The cabinet committee closed its doors on December 30, 1974. Its good intentions were not enough to achieve its pledge to mitigate poverty among U.S. Hispanics. It did not affect Mexican American nor Puerto Rican poverty rates. Neither did it affect underachieving public schools, nor high unemployment rates. But it did create jobs for a few political activists and presented an image that it helped poor people, even if its reality was quite different.

President Nixon also appointed other Mexican Americans from Los Angeles to top positions in his administration, most notably Ramona Banuelos as U.S. Treasurer. Years later, in August, 2001, President George W. Bush appointed Rosario Marin of Huntington Park as U.S. Treasurer. These appointees, however, were more engaged in Republican Party-building than in energizing U.S. Hispanic communities to develop independent political power across the nation.

Church Engagement

Protestant church denominations in Los Angeles both initiated and sponsored social justice projects for Mexican Americans. They maintained a tradition of operating programs concerned exclusively with Hispanic ministries. They also initiated programs to prepare Mexican American congregations to go beyond a "survival mentality" and to form a new self-image for "authentic" evangelism and liberating social action.[28]

The Catholic church, likewise, began to address problems of the poor more vigorously after the 1965 Second Vatican Council. It encouraged Catholics to design ways to deal with changes in the modern world. It acknowledged a desire by lay members to participate more fully in church life. It motivated Central American bishops to declare a "preferential option for the poor" in the work of the church and set free a spirit of liberation among the church of the poor.

Fr. Ralph Ramirez of San Antonio sparked formation in 1968 of *Padres Asociados Para Derechos Religiosos Educativos y Sociales* (PADRES), a national association of Chicano Catholic priests. Its Second National Congress met in Los Angeles in October 1971 and expanded its membership in Los Angeles. PADRES spoke out for social justice in solidarity with the Mexican American people. It aimed to make religious services more relevant through use of the Spanish language, respect for cultural traditions, and appointment of Mexican American bishops. It helped establish the Mexican American Cultural Center (MACC) in San Antonio in 1972, the first national institute to train priests as well as religious and lay leaders for missions to local communities. It also promoted concepts of liberation theology. Its members participated in community campaigns to empower the poor for self-development.[29]

Mexican American religious women formed an association called *Las Hermanas* (The Sisters) that advocated for a more active church role in people's daily struggles for cultural retention and social justice. They opposed racism where it occurred, even inside the Catholic Church.[30] From the perspective of some Chicano movement activists, however, the Catholic Church changed too slowly.[31]

In Los Angeles, during the fall of 1969, a Chicano activist group took a new direction and clashed directly with officials of the Catholic Church. Moises Sandoval, author and editor of Maryknoll magazine, traced origins of the conflict to a decision by church officials to close Our Lady Queen of Angeles High School, a Catholic girl's high school attended mostly by Mexican Americans.[32] A small group of Chicano college students decided to oppose the closure. They met with church officials who insisted that a lack of funds necessitated the closure. The activist group remained unconvinced in the light of an ambitious, ongoing building program in other areas of the city at the same time.

The impasse with Church officials led activists to form a group called *Catolicos Por La Raza* (CPLR), led by Richard Cruz.[33] It demanded Church involvement in the Chicano struggle for better schools, affordable housing, support for the UFW grape strike, and opposition to the Vietnam War and racism. CPLR accelerated its campaign at a press conference reported by the Los Angeles Times, which called on the Catholic Church to relate more to the Mexican American people in Los Angeles.[34] It demanded that the Church stop charging tuition for parochial schools and that it subsidize the educational expenses of all Chicano students in high school and college.

On December 7, 1969, CPLR members protested what they called church indifference in front of St. Basil's Church, home of James Francis Cardinal McIntyre, Archbishop of Los Angeles. Then on December 18, thirty CPLR members showed up at the main church office and demanded to speak to Cardinal McIntyre. The meeting polarized both sides and resulted in heightened tension between them.[35]

On Christmas Eve, 1969, Los Angeles police arrested CPLR activists for disturbing the yearly televised midnight mass at St. Basil's church downtown. I attended the demonstration because of my conviction that the church should help us fight injustice. Most of us who went there remained outside the church. I, and others, disagreed with a planned intrusion into the church ceremony and left. A televised disturbance with off-screen sounds shocked viewing Catholics in Los Angeles. The arrested demonstrators subsequently asked for forgiveness – a very Christian concept -- but the law ran its course.[36] Three Chicano men, an Anglo woman, and a former nun were convicted of disturbing the peace and sentenced to jail terms of one to four months, while one Chicana served three years probation.[37] The public controversy, arrests, trials, and ongoing protests, including the burning of baptismal certificates in front of St. Basil's Church,[38] signaled growing tension in the relationship between the Church and the Mexican American people in Los Angeles[39] that spilled over into San Diego.[40]

CPLR coordinated protest activities from the Euclid Community Center in Boyle Heights, where anti-war activities were also planned, and its actions continued for over a year. A popular CPLR slogan and chant was "The church belongs to the people." However, its original goal of saving the girls high school was not met. Despite the fact that CPLR had widespread movement activist support, including that of the Congress of Mexican American Unity, the masses of Mexican Americans active in the Catholic Church -- particularly parishes in East Los Angeles -- rejected CPLR and its demands.[41]

Without noticeable support inside the Catholic Church or resources to sustain a long-term campaign, CPLR faded away. The State Committee of Bar Examiners held back CPLR leader Richard Cruz from practicing law for two years after he passed the State Bar examination. Eventually, Roman Catholic Bishop Juan Arzube testified on his behalf at a bar committee hearing, and Cruz was finally admitted to the California bar in April, 1973.[42]

The high profile but brief existence of CPLR demonstrates how small groups in the heat of larger social movements can generate events, rhetoric, and publicity to influence construction of a fluid movement ideology. It illustrates how small transitory activist groups with righteous anger can position themselves prominently inside a larger movement for an intense, if brief, period of time. As a result of CPLR's work, Chicano activists expanded the movement "enemy list" to include non-responsive established churches.

Chapter 7

Mass Protest

By now, the anti-war mass protest became a full blown social movement across America that further agitated Chicano activists. Anger and frustration with the war were at a high point. In the face of higher U.S. casualties, even though President Nixon announced the first withdrawal of U.S. troops from Vietnam, the U.S. military secretly bombed Cambodia. Around this time, the U.S. military said that Vietnamese villages had to be destroyed to "save" them and anti-war sentiments reached the troops in Vietnam. Americans heard for the first time about "fragging," frontline slang for U.S. troops shooting their own officers in battle. News of the failing war and the massive anti-war movement dominated television screens at home.

In Los Angeles, during the same summer, the heated national anti-war movement absorbed Chicano activists. Rosalio Munoz, for example, refused to be inducted for the draft in order to protest poverty and racism, and he began a hunger strike against the war.[1][2] He also traveled up and down the state to help form the National Chicano Moratorium Committee, coinciding with a call for National Moratorium Days by peace activists across the country. The Chicano Moratorium Committee operated out of the Euclid Community Center in Boyle Heights, where the Educational Issues Coordinating Committee (EICC) also held its meetings. The center became a clearinghouse for Chicano anti-war information and planned demonstrations.

The Chicano anti-war agenda in Los Angeles included opposition to second-rate schools at home. Los Angeles school board member Julian Nava won a fight for public disclosure of reading scores on a school-by-school basis. As a result, for the first time parents found out which schools had low reading scores. As expected, schools in minority areas scored below the national average and at least two grades behind all-Anglo schools in Los Angeles.[3]

Angry Chicano activists demanded that teachers and principals be transferred out of schools with low scores or be fired.[4] School district officials responded in part with funding for bilingual education programs, but dropout rates remained high. And despite their best efforts, Mexican American school parents continued to be shut out of meaningful participation in decision-making about personnel, budget, and curricula in the education of their own children.

The national anti-war movement resulted in the first actual withdrawal of U.S. troops from Vietnam in July,1969, and the cancellation of draft calls for November and December. Nonetheless, more frequent and larger anti-war demonstrations took place in major U.S. cities. The anti-war and Civil Rights Movements together reached into all sectors of U.S. society, including Catholic and Protestant churches. Churches of all denominations also opposed the war in Vietnam. Major church denominations committed themselves to oppose racism, economic exploitation, and degradation of Mexican Americans in society.

By now, at least a third of the American people wanted U.S. troops to come home alive, not as televised body counts. But student unrest on college campuses also became a national concern. A Gallup Poll published on June 19, 1970, reported that Americans named campus unrest as the nation's number one problem, eclipsing even such problems as the Vietnam War and racial strife. At the same time, police officers across the country continued to use tear gas to break up peace demonstrations. In the late 1960's, the U.S. government prepared contingency plans for intervention in civil disturbances. Now it was ready to deal directly with civil unrest.[5] Even so, anti-war activists continued to protest.

In Los Angeles, Chicano movement activists, mostly the Brown Berets and the Chicano Moratorium Committee, agitated for a quicker end to the war, even though it was already winding down. They reached out to activists in other states for coordinated protests. On February 28, 1970, over 3,000 activists -- mostly from California with contingents from Colorado, New Mexico, and Texas -- marched in the rain in East Los Angeles to protest the high casualty rate of Chicanos in Vietnam.[6] Marchers proclaimed that the battle ground for social justice was not in Vietnam, but in the United States.

In the meantime, the UFW campaign for collective bargaining in California moved ahead. In 1969, its boycott of California grapes led to direct negotiations with California growers. Time Magazine featured Cesar Chavez on its cover with a major article on the UFW strike as "*la causa*" or social movement of the Mexican American people.[7] In 1970, Newsweek also took note of the "*movimiento Chicano*" and described it as a symbolic killing of "*Tio Taco*," (Uncle Taco), a stereotype of a lazy Mexican American without ambition.[8] It described a new social movement seeking to define itself and its goals, where Mexican Americans lived in significant numbers.

But on December 4, 1970, Cesar Chavez was jailed for refusing to stop the campaign to boycott lettuce farms. He cited constitutional rights and refused to obey a court injunction obtained by the Dow Chemical Company against the boycott.[9] Chicano movement activists supported Chavez and the UFW in spite of this emergence of a powerful enemy.

Activists also identified the film industry as a new movement enemy. In 1970, *Justicia*, a group in El Sereno led by Ray Andrade, distributed a 16-page report that identified racism and job bias against Chicanos in the film and television industries.[10] The report complained of racial stereotypes, like images of the Frito Bandito, Jose Jimenez, and Speedy Gonzalez. It objected to the Hollywood version of a Chicano accent, like "my seester" and "I teenk." It also protested a failure to report on degrading social conditions affecting the Chicano people. *Justicia* charged that the film industry perpetuated an image of Mexicans as stupid and lazy along with a myth of white supremacy. It objected to glorification of violence against Mexicans, especially in movies like "Butch Cassidy and The Sundance Kid" and "The Wild Bunch."[11]

In April, 1970, 250 movement activists led by Thomas Martinez protested with a noisy demonstration at the annual Academy Awards ceremony at the Dorothy Chandler Pavilion in downtown Los Angeles. They heckled movie industry figures, including John Wayne, and protested racist Western movies that demeaned Chicanos with images of white supremacy.[12] *Justicia* and other groups, including *Nosotros,* a group focused on improving the image of Latinos in the entertainment industry, continued to monitor both on camera and behind the scenes film and television industry performance.[13] They demanded realistic portrayals with dignity and respect of Chicano culture, language, and history. They also insisted on equal opportunity for Chicanos in the broadcast media in writing, acting, and producing programs.

La Raza Unida Party

Some Chicano movement groups added the Democratic and Republican parties to the enemies list. They called for Chicanos to break away from both parties with their own third party.[14] During the 1970 elections, they attempted to register enough voters to form an official Chicano political party to be called *La Raza Unida Party.*

I reregistered as member of this new party. Even though it was unable to win an election, it sustained strong criticism among activists of the failure of both Democratic and Republican parties to address problems of Mexican American families.

La Raza Unida did win elections in Crystal City, Texas, a small rural town. The local victories, led by Jose Angel Gutierrez, inspired party members to plan for a national Chicano political party. In California, *La Raza Unida* recruited cadres of highly motivated university students to help form the new party throughout the state.[15] They initiated voter registration campaigns on college campuses, in front of large markets, and at community events wherever people gathered.

In Los Angeles, the new political party also used direct action approaches to community problems. During May 1972, it picketed the Million Dollar Theater downtown to protest racism in the form of overpriced admission tickets and a need for building repairs. The 6-week protest led to police confrontations and arrests, but the pickets won all of their demands.[16] A year later, those arrested won a clear victory in court when they had all charges dismissed.[17]

Over the next few years, however, the new Chicano political party could not generate enough registered members to become an electoral threat. It lacked sufficient resources, prominent endorsements, extensive publicity, and experienced campaign managers. The Congress of Mexican American Unity (CMAU), for example endorsed Democrats for public office, but only a few *La Raza Unida* candidates. Even the Mexican American Political Association (MAPA) consistently aligned itself with Democratic candidates. Occasionally it endorsed a Republican or a third party nominee, such as Peace and Freedom Party candidate Ricardo Romo for Governor in 1970, but it evaded endorsement of La Raza Unida candidate.

Electoral defeats nonetheless became rhetorical victories for the new political party. Some activists, for example, pointed with honor to participation in "losing causes."[18] Since the new political party achieved its goal of raising political consciousness, it interpreted losses as symbols of future victories.[19] Still, the hard work of organizing a viable and independent political party for Chicanos has remained an unfulfilled goal.[20]

In 1970, Chicano movement events helped accelerate more mass protest demonstrations. This new wave of action was fired up by movement newspapers, including *La Vida Nueva*, a student publication at East Los Angeles College, and *El Machete*, at Los Angeles City College. These important movement publications expressed support for farm workers and Chicano candidates for political office. They disseminated news about defense committees, police occupation of the barrio, inferior schools, Chicano prison inmates, the changing role of women in the movement, and the war. Community college student newspapers increased demands for social justice sand became an important voice in the growing awareness of movement issues.

Police Abuse

Activists responded directly to police abuse. On the Fourth of July, 1970, a coalition of Chicano movement groups protested police abuse at a rally. Student members of *Movimiento Estudiantil Chicano de Aztlan* (MECHA) at Cal State LA, the Brown Berets, the Chicano Moratorium Committee, and the Barrio Defense Committee together protested the suspicious deaths within the past year of six Chicano prisoners at the East Los Angeles sheriff's station. They gathered at Belvedere Park near the sheriff's station and announced that, like American revolutionaries, they too declared their own independence from an abusive police force that occupied their community. They blamed community anger at injustice for a "mini-riot" of July 3rd that resulted in damage to 35 stores in East Los Angeles and 26 arrests.[21]

A following protest demonstration by 350 activists took place on Friday, July 11, 1970, in front of the East Los Angeles sheriff's station. Protestors included members of the Congress of Mexican American Unity (CMAU), *Movimiento Estudiantil Chicano de Aztlan* (MECHA), Mexican American Political Association (MAPA), American GI Forum, Chicano Moratorium Committee, Barrio Defense Committee, and League of United Citizens to Help Addicts (LUCHA). They demanded an official investigation of police arrests and abuses related to the riot of July 3. They also warned that unchecked police violence would beget violence in return. They pledged to unite 300 Chicano organizations in Los Angeles County to stop police harassment.[22]

Within a week, on the night of July 16, 1970, five Los Angeles policemen and two detectives from San Leandro entered an apartment on east Seventh Street near downtown in search of a murder suspect. They found six innocent unarmed Mexican nationals and killed two of them, cousins Beltran and Guillermo Sanchez. At a press conference the following day, the police acknowledged they made a mistake. The next day, Saturday, July 18, Gloria Chavez of *Catolicos Por La Raza* (CPLR) and Rosalio Munoz of the Chicano Moratorium Committee led 350 Chicanos in a protest march in front of police headquarters downtown. They demanded justice and warned that innocent Chicano families were no longer safe from police assassins in their own homes.

Other movement groups joined protest demonstrations during the following week. Congressman Edward R. Roybal called for a shakeup in the police department, creation of an appeal board for citizen complaints against police abuse, and a grand jury investigation. The District Attorney filed criminal charges against the involved police officers.[23]

On August 6, 1970, another protest march took place against police abuse. The Chicano Moratorium Committee, The East Los Angeles Community Union (TELACU), and the Congress of Mexican American Unity (CMAU) organized a memorial protest march over the killing of the Sanchez cousins. The number of marchers, joined by the Brown Berets, increased to almost 900 from the time they left the corner of Brooklyn Avenue (now Cesar Chavez Avenue) and Indiana Avenue in East Los Angeles.

At the protest rally at the Los Angeles police headquarters downtown, Esteban Torres, Oscar Acosta, Rosalio Munoz, and the Brown Berets accused the police of practicing genocide, and demanded the resignation of Los Angeles Police Chief Edward Davis. They urged movement activists to engage in day-to-day organizing to reach more people. They also warned against forming movement elites or of making the movement something for an "in-crowd."[25]

Chicano Moratorium Committee

Activists in the Chicano Moratorium Committee, led by Rosalio Munoz, now became more prominent with an anti-war campaign and condemnation of anti-Chicano racism. The Committee mobilized and consolidated Chicano groups in the Southwest for a large anti-war protest march in East Los Angeles. Even though the national anti-war movement was ending, the Committee anticipated thousands of marchers in Los Angeles to demonstrate national Chicano opposition to the war.[25]

The Chicano Moratorium Committee radicalized other anti-war protest groups as it aimed to educate Chicanos about the "true nature" of the war and the disproportionate death rate of Chicanos in Vietnam. It also objected to police abuse, racism, and suppression of free speech at home. It scheduled the local march to follow prior marches in Houston, San Diego, Oakland, and Los Angeles. In the process, it reaffirmed the importance of large mass protest events to recruit new movement participants.

On August 29, 1970, a strong sense of solidarity fortified the marchers. I participated with a contingency of Head Start teachers, parents and children. We marched proudly among an estimated twenty thousand men, women and children who represented groups from throughout the Southwest. Marchers shouted in unison, "Brown Power!" We paraded in long files that filled the streets from sidewalk to sidewalk, south on Atlantic Boulevard and west on Whittier Boulevard. The main streets of East Los Angeles were lined with a variety of storefronts, bars and cafes, fast-food restaurants, auto dealerships, St. Alphonsus Catholic Church, and medical offices, and people poured out to cheer us on, often stepping off the sidewalks to join us.

An animated small group that marched directly behind ours kept cadence with shouts like "Worker Power!" and "*Capitalismo No! Socialismo Si!*" and waved small red flags. Other marchers shouted cadences of "*Chale con la draft!*" (No to the draft), "*Raza Si! Guerra No!*" (People yes, War no), and "Chicano Power!" Our chants pumped enthusiasm all along the long line of marchers and large crowds along the sidewalk. Marchers waved yellow, blue, green, and red hand-held signs, banners, U.S. and Mexican flags, and UFW flags with a black eagle on a red background. Contingents of college and high school students, labor unions, civic groups, civil rights activists, political groups, and religious people enlivened the march with loud rhythmic yells and anti-war, anti-draft slogans, like the familiar "Hell No! We Won't Go!"

Thousands of people along the streets applauded the three hour march, and many of the spectators joined the column, even elderly people and young "homeboys and homegirls." It was truly a serious and expressive people's march that ended with a rally at Laguna Park. The park filled up rapidly with tired but enthusiastic men, women, young marchers, and children. Many marchers joined families who waited for them in the park.

Our group sat at the edge of the park, on the warm lawn under the hot sun where we could hear musicians sing Mexican songs and speakers on a stage who denounced police repression, racism, the draft, and the Vietnam War. Rosalie Gurrola, a Head Start teacher, and I decided to buy sodas at a nearby liquor store for relief from thirst and the hot summer weather. Inside the crowded store, we heard the owner complain of too many customers at one time as he telephoned someone for help.

A large number of Los Angeles county deputy sheriffs and Los Angeles City policemen were ready. Busloads of backup law enforcement officers appeared in full riot uniforms within minutes. The combined county and city police forces stationed themselves at the park's edge and with a bull horn ordered the rally to stop immediately. Most people could not hear the order to evacuate the park. When the anti-war and anti-police speakers continued, the joint city police and county sheriffs forces formed a line across the width of the park and entered to vacate it by force.

Rosalie Gurrola and I were standing across the street from the park when a White deputy sheriff waving a police baton came towards us. I saw hatred in his eyes as we turned to walk away and he turned to walk into the park to strike others with his baton. I felt a strong sense of outrage at police violation of our constitutional rights of free assembly and free speech for all marchers and rally participants.

73

The police decision to evacuate the park by force turned out to be either a gross police tactical error or an intentional attack on peaceful people, since the police line blocked the park main exit. Families in the park got trapped between back fences and the line of approaching city police and county sheriffs. The main way out of the park necessitated getting past the line of police and sheriffs officers with batons.

We saw an advancing phalanx of helmeted policemen and deputy sheriffs swinging clubs at people who had become trapped in the park, forcing some to fight back. As fights with policemen broke out, bottles were thrown and in response, police tear gas canisters exploded. People ran in different directions through police lines, some with blood on their faces. Parents shouted and screamed for their children, and children cried in fear, separated from their parents, as the situation escalated into a full blown police-community riot. It resulted in three deaths, the arrest of over 140 people, and extensive damage to business property. It confirmed for activists the racism and police brutality the march was designed to protest.

Ruben Salazar

During the police-community riot, a deputy sheriff shot and killed Ruben Salazar, 42, a well-known KMEX-TV newscaster and Los Angeles Times columnist who covered Chicano protest events in Los Angeles and was on assignment at the time. Salazar had already been under FBI surveillance for his travels in Central America and his newspaper articles in support of the Chicano anti-war movement. A coroner's inquest into his death featured dramatic testimony and photos taken by *La Raza* magazine co-editors Raul Ruiz and Joe Razo. The photos showed a deputy sheriff armed and poised with an unauthorized anti-barricade missile launcher ready to shoot at chest level into the Silver Dollar Café. Salazar sat inside the bar on Whittier Boulevard, away from the scattering crowd, separated from smoke clouds, burning automobiles, and buildings, and relieved of the summer heat, when a large missile to his head killed him instantly. The coroner's jury found that Salazar had died "at the hands of another."

Los Angeles District Attorney Evelle J. Younger, however, refused to believe that his death was intentional and declined to file criminal charges. Salazar, who a year earlier predicted his fate in a speech in San Antonio, became a martyr for the Chicano movement.[26] Four thousand people attended his funeral in East Los Angeles. County sheriffs stayed away from the funeral at the request of the family to avoid confrontation with community activists.[27] President Nixon sent a letter of condolence to his family and Robert Finch, counselor to the President, attended the funeral.[28]

A month before his death, Salazar wrote in his newspaper column how two policemen visited him to complain about his reports on the police shooting and killing in 1970 of two innocent cousins, unarmed Mexican nationals, in Los Angeles.[29] The policemen warned him of the negative impact his reports had on the police department's image. The warning, however, served to make him more determined to write about police misconduct and abuse. He refused to be intimidated.[30]

Suspicion lingered that, like President John Kennedy, U.S. Senator Robert Kennedy, and Rev. Martin Luther King, Jr., Salazar might have been assassinated.[31] Attorney Oscar Acosta, for example, charged the County sheriffs department with conspiracy to murder Salazar.[32] Community groups, including Manual Ruiz Jr., a Los Angeles attorney and member of the U.S. Commission On Civil Rights, demanded a federal probe.

A federal grand jury was convened to examine the case, but their inquiry failed to issue indictments. Nonetheless, in 1973, Salazar's family received over $700,000 in settlement of a wrongful death lawsuit against Los Angeles County. A later examination of Federal Bureau of Investigation files under the Freedom of Information Act revealed that the FBI had been tracking Salazar for three years, especially his travels as a journalist to Cuba, the Dominican Republic, and South Vietnam.[33]

Salazar's death and the riot became like a trumpet blast that summoned people to a holy war and gained new recruits to the Chicano movement. Government officials changed the name of Laguna Park, where the police assault began, to Ruben Salazar Park in his memory. Chicano faculty and students at Cal State LA, in East Los Angeles succeeded in naming a classroom building Salazar Hall, and scholarships carried his name. Buildings were also named in his honor in other locations. After the riot and Salazar's death, most Mexican American civic groups fell in line behind the movement.

At the same time, law enforcement officers continued to harass members of the Chicano movement. The Chicano Moratorium Committee and the Congress of Mexican American Unity (CMAU) joined the East Los Angeles Mexican Independence Day parade on September 16, 1970.[34] This traditional festive march of over 200,000 marchers and spectators was mostly peaceful. The moratorium contingent protested inferior schools, police brutality, anti-immigrant government practices, and a degrading welfare system.

But last-minute confusion about arrangements with the Los Angeles Junior College Board of Trustees triggered another violent confrontation between police and marchers. The ending of the parade disintegrated into chaos after cancellation of permission to use East Los Angeles College Stadium for a post-march rally. Violence erupted as the day turned into night, resulting in three people shot, more than 100 injured, and 68 arrested.[35]

In the meantime, Chicano activists expressed disappointment with civic groups that had not declared open support for movement protests and events. Movement activists considered civic groups as either in or out of the movement, with no allowance for fence sitters. The Barrio Defense Committee, led by Celia L. de Rodriguez,[36] pressed grievances against police harassment, including defense of Corky Gonzales, who was arrested during the East L.A. riot. The Barrio Defense Committee joined the Congress of Mexican American Unity (CMAU) and the Chicano Moratorium Committee to condemn continuing police harassment.

During November 1970, the Chicano Moratorium Committee conducted a Saturday morning picket line against police abuse in front of the Hollenbeck police station in Boyle Heights. It contin-ued the picketing in spite of a police raid of the office of the Chicano Moratorium Committee on November 14, which resulted in the arrest of three activists.

The Chicano Moratorium Committee called for a mass protest demonstration to show solidarity with the 52 activists who had been ar-rested, some of them beaten, by Los Angeles police for protest activities. It vowed not to back down from demands for justice and to show that *La Raza* was not afraid of the police. On Saturday, January 9, 1971, sev-eral hundred people joined in a demonstration that began with a 1:00 p.m. assembly at Hollenbeck Park in Boyle Heights. They marched to nearby Hollenbeck police station, picketed around the premises, then marched on the sidewalk to police headquarters downtown. Along the way, confrontations with police took place, and several protest marchers were arrested.[37]

By the time the marchers arrived at police headquarters, they numbered almost 1,000, including several hundred Anglos. Officers surrounded the police building and, after some skirmishes, they de-clared an unlawful assembly and ordered the protestors to leave. Some protestors refused to move and fought back. A contingent of protes-tors then ran six blocks down Broadway Street though downtown and smashed the windows of more than 20 businesses.

The protest march and ensuing problems resulted in the arrest of 36 Chicano movement activists, minor injuries to a score of police, and property damage. After this mass demonstration, Los Angeles Police Chief Edward Davis made a widely publicized declaration that blamed anti-police protests on wealthy "swimming pool Communists" who avoided arrest, and Brown Berets who exploited young Mexican Americans into forming a revolutionary movement.

On January 23, 1971, the Los Angeles Times published a letter to the editor by Rosalio Munoz, leader of the Chicano Moratorium Committee.[38] He said that in spite of police-initiated political violence against them, Chicanos would continue to protest injustice as a strategy to help their community survive as a people. In the meantime, movement activists continued plans for a massive demonstration against police repression and brutality in East Los Angeles.[39] [40]

On January 31, 1971, the Chicano Moratorium Committee held a major protest demonstration against police brutality and the Vietnam War. It gathered approximately 4,000 people at Belvedere Park in East Los Angeles. Movement groups that arrived from Pomona, Long Beach, San Pedro, Santa Ana, La Puente, and the San Fernando Valley added much excitement when their separate arrivals were announced at the park. Along the way, they conducted rolling peaceful demonstrations in front of police, sheriff, and California Highway Patrol offices. Even though Belvedere Park was near a sheriff's office, the sheriffs kept a low profile and remained out of sight during the rally. Moratorium Committee planners and monitors, with the help of the Brown Berets, preserved a peaceful atmosphere.[41]

The rally ended peacefully at 3:00 in the afternoon. But immediately afterwards, about 1,000 Chicano youth, perhaps including some possible agents' provocateurs, turned to violence and wrecked the Moratorium Committee's intended peaceful event. A group of young people tore down a chain link fence around a sheriff's parking lot and broke car windows. They moved to Whittier Boulevard and smashed windows in stores and office buildings, looted stores, set off a series of fires, and threw rocks and bottles at fire fighters. The disturbance spread to other streets and fire bombs hit buildings until the sheriff deputies responded in force.[42]

The young Chicanos threw rocks, bottles, and chunks of cement at deputies, who fired warning shots into the air.[43] The riot caused the death of Gustav Montage Jr., 24, from El Sereno, hit by a possible ricocheting bullet in a fight between 40 young Chicanos and sheriff deputies. The riot also resulted in injury to 37 people, 11 of them sheriff's deputies. Ninety men, women, and juveniles were arrested. Twelve sheriff's cars and one California Highway Patrol car were damaged. More than 80 stores sustained damage, including six cars at an automobile agency. Rosalio Munoz of the moratorium committee blamed the deputy sheriffs for provoking the riot,[44] but a Los Angles Times editorial called for a moratorium on Chicano Moratoriums.[45]

The Moratorium Committee changed strategy from organizing one-day events to events of a longer duration in order to politicize people on a larger scale.[46] It organized the *Marcha de la Reconquista*, (March of the Reconquest), a protest march that began in Calexico on the Mexican border on May 5, 1971. Rosalio Munoz and Gil Cano led a core group of 60 people on a three-month march north for 800 miles. Along the way, they urged people to join the movement for justice and to register as members of *La Raza Unida* Party. The Brown Berets protected them as they marched along highways and through city streets.

The marchers arrived in Los Angeles in mid-June and reached Sacramento on August 7. At the capitol, they held protest demonstrations for a week aimed at anti-Chicano policies of Governor Ronald Reagan and his administration. The protestors demanded reforms in welfare, changes in the system of corrections, better work conditions for farm workers, protection of immigrant families, and an end to the war. The marchers called their march a symbol of the willingness of the Chicano people to sacrifice for justice.[47]

In addition to its supporters, the Chicano movement attracted enemies both outside and inside the movement. In the case of the Chicano Moratorium Committee, an enemy came in the form of an alleged "agent provocateur" and police informer. Frank Martinez, a militant activist who claimed to speak for the Moratorium Committee from November 1970 to March 1971, was alleged to be a police agent. He was alleged to have used extremist language of violence, to have advocated illegal acts, and to have setup a police raid of the Moratorium Committee office.[48] Movement groups remained on high alert for possible police infiltrators who, once discovered, disappeared.

In retrospect, the work of the Chicano Moratorium Committee gave full expression to righteous anger at injustice, created drama, had major protest events, released expressive energy, achieved symbolic conquest over enemies, and polarized movement followers against outsiders. It also made clear that Chicano groups could unite for major demonstrations, and to push demands for social justice both inside and outside existing social institutions.[49]

But like other movement groups, the Moratorium Committee was unable to control a fringe of violent activists that joined its demonstrations and made the whole movement appear violent. Some movement leaders themselves recognized the limits of organizing that centered on more militant activists. They sensed a need to organize for permanent power among neighborhood families and working poor that formed the life and blood of the community.[50]

Even so, the Moratorium Committee created a great momentum that involved thousands of people in a new political consciousness and solidarity. It left a proud legacy of Chicano collective anger at injustice, boosted cultural identity, and underscored the determination to struggle for social justice.

Yet, as always, fundamental problems remained of crushing poverty and political disenfranchisement for immigrants and the working poor.

Prison Outreach

By 1970, the movement and protest marches in Los Angeles included "*pintos*" and "*batos locos*," popular names given to Chicano prison inmates, ex-convicts, and rowdy young men. The prison was "*la pinta*" and a prisoner a "*pinto*." At that time, Chicanos comprised only 10 percent of the state population but 20 percent of all inmates in prison. Many Chicano ex-convicts became street-wise and survived against the odds. They lacked political power, but nonetheless energized the movement as anti-establishment boosters.[51]

Chicano *pintos* thought of themselves as political prisoners, and organized movement groups in state prisons, such as *El Mexicano Preparado Listo Educado Organizado* (EMPLEO) in San Quentin prison, *Chicanos*

Organizado Pintos de Aztlan (COPA) in Chino prison, and *Movimiento Aztlan Chicano Organizado* (MACHO) in Tehachapi state prison. They also formed groups outside of prison, like the League of United Citizens to Help Addicts (LUCHA) led by Eduardo Aguirre, an ex-convict from East Los Angeles. The plight of Chicano prisoners and ex-convicts in the criminal justice system became part of the stated concerns of the movement.[52]

Headquartered in East Los Angeles, LUCHA supported the UFW and local protest demonstrations. Its goal was to help men and women withdraw from drug addiction. It circulated a citizen's initiative petition for signatures of registered voters. The initiative, entitled a "People's Resolution For Penal Reform," was to be submitted to California voters for adoption. It aimed to transfer all laws concerning drug addiction from the Penal Code to the Welfare and Institution Codes. The purpose was to reclassify non-violent drug abuse as a health issue, not criminal, and at the same time reduce the number of prisoners in state jails. It blamed lack of jobs, poverty and bad schools as the main evils in Chicano communities. It also attempted to secure public funding, but was unsuccessful. After a brief period of intense movement activity, LUCHA, like other movement groups, drifted away.

In 1969, the state mandated admission of minority students to California colleges. The program organized to assist students on campus became the Equal Opportunity Program (EOP). It also established off-campus college programs for Chicanos in state prisons. The goal was to make educational opportunities available to state prisoners with the cooperation of the California Department of Corrections.[53]

As a faculty member in the Chicano Studies Department, I taught introductory Chicano Studies college courses at the Tehachapi and Chino state prisons for men, the federal Terminal Island prison in San Pedro, the California Institution For Women at Frontera, and at the California Youth Authority Facility for young men in Chino. Inmate students showed a serious attitude and attentiveness. They welcomed me and occasional small groups of visiting students with courtesy and encouraged us to make more prison visits.

Urban Development

Social protest in East Los Angeles also elicited reaction from governmental agencies. The federally funded Model Cities program in Los Angeles was reorganized in 1970 to put the mayor and city council in direct charge of all anti-poverty programs. It created Residents Councils in Mexican American and Black poverty neighborhoods.[54] I served as Chairman of the City Demonstration Agency Board (CDA), as Model Cities was called in the Eastside. But by 1974, the Model Cities program had become part of the regular city bureaucracy.[55]

During its span of existence and millions of dollars spent, movement groups mistrusted the Model Cities program. They demanded an elected Model Cities board of directors to represent community residents instead of a board appointed by elected officials. This demand was often repeated in Chicano movement discourse. Mayor Sam Yorty, however, ignored the request for an elected board. As a result, to protest the lack of local community elections, in April of 1972, I resigned from the CDA board.

Two years later, the Model Cities program was over. Like the War on Poverty, it had some success. It funded some worthwhile programs, like the One-Stop Immigration Center in Boyle Heights, and created jobs for hundreds of residents. But at the same time, it failed to reduce poverty rates in the Mexican American community. In fact, during its time of operation, poverty got worse.

Confrontations continued to occur between local residents and government officials over city and county plans for economic and housing development in East Los Angeles. Victories won by activists in some of those confrontations revealed a potential to organize homeowners and residents for self-defense. Residents, mostly Mexican American who lived in the unincorporated City Terrace neighborhood of East

Los Angeles, faced the threat of unwanted development. A community campaign in Boyle Heights, Lincoln Heights, and El Sereno put an end to a city-sponsored Housing Development Corporation plan to replace existing homes with new ones.

Chicano movement activists usually ignored the organizing opportunity inherent in church-based groups. However, in City Terrace, I led a group of students that went door to door to inquire as to what residents knew about county plans for redevelopment. We discovered that they were uniformed, uninvolved, uninvited, and unwelcome in local planning decisions.[56] A group of local residents, assisted by Rosalio Munoz, formed to oppose these county development plans. The group met with leaders of a faith-based action group called *Cursillo* (activist religious group) at St. Lucy's Catholic Church in City Terrace. *Cursillo* leaders feared for the older retired people, who would die if relocated far from their routine lives and friends. They put their religious faith to work to protect families and their homes from harm. They explained the issue to worshipers outside after masses on Sunday.

On the morning of March 21, 1973, they filled the hearing room of the Regional Planning Commission in the Hall of Administration downtown with 500 residents to protest county redevelopment plans. Speakers at the hearing opposed over-zoning and high density apartment projects in the area. They won a commitment from the county planning commission to work with residents on a separate balanced plan for the area.[57] [58] The victory resulted in a more influential role for local residents in the planning process as it demonstrated the organizing potential of church leaders and their families.

Immigrant Defense

Since the massive deportations of Mexican immigrant families during the Great Depression, when immigrants were blamed for unemployment, Chicano activists in Los Angeles have defended Mexican immigrant workers and their families. Both native-born and undocumented

Mexican workers experienced discrimination and exploitation on the job, and faced racist treatment in society. They were denied fair and humane treatment by federal, state, and local governments. Activists defended immigrant families and workers through the work of civil rights organizations, labor unions in the garment industry and service trades and nonprofit foundations, as well as churches and religious groups. Those groups also fought against deportations of immigrant workers.

Activists formed organizations with the specific goal of immigrant defense. *La Hermandad de Trabajadores*, led by Bert Corona, defended undocumented immigrants in Los Angeles. It also conducted classes to prepare Spanish-speaking undocumented immigrants for citizenship applications. Another prominent Chicano movement organization that defended immigrant families was *Centro de Accion Social Autonoma* (CASA), led by Antonio Rodriguez. CASA combined defense of immigrant workers with anti-war and anti-police abuse demonstrations. It had chapters in several cities and became the foremost immigrant defense organization in the Los Angeles Mexican American community.[59]

CASA published a newspaper called *Sin Fronteras* (Without Borders), edited by Carlos Vasquez. It presented perspectives on U.S. immigration policy and relations with Mexico. It also called for unification of the Mexican people in the United States and Mexico without regard to borders. CASA became a cornerstone organization of the Chicano movement, with a popular base of support and growing influence in regional opposition to U.S. immigration policy. Defense of undocumented immigrant workers became a major issue for all movement activists.

Meanwhile, the Chicano Law Students Association in Los Angeles was formed in support of a growing number of movement organizations. In November, 1970, it published *Justicia O!* (Justice Or), a bilingual newspaper dedicated to equal justice before the courts and in the administration of justice for the Mexican American people. FBI director J. Edgar Hoover created doubts of a fair administration of justice for Mexican Americans when he called them people "prone to assault you with a knife." In response, in December, 1970, Congressman Edward R. Roybal demanded Hoover's resignation for making slurs against people of Mexican and Puerto Rican descent.[60]

In the meantime, *Regeneracion*, a new movement publication edited by Francisca Flores, appeared in East Los Angeles. It disseminated movement information to a large cross-section of readers and included articles on electoral campaigns, the war, police brutality, the schools, racism against Chicanos, as well as book reviews, poetry, and photographs.

During 1971 and 1972, as the Brown Berets and the Chicano Moratorium Committee escalated Chicano social protest with a series of anti-war demonstrations in East Los Angeles, a desperate individual act took over the drama of protest against U.S. racism. Ricardo Chavez-Ortiz, 37, was a Mexican immigrant worker who lived with his wife and eight children in a small house on Cummings Street in Boyle Heights. The house faced a concrete wall alongside the Santa Ana Freeway, south of First Street.

On April 13, 1972, deeply concerned over racism against Mexican immigrants, Chavez-Ortiz took over a Frontier Airlines twin-engine Boeing 737 short-range jet with 27 passengers and six crew members on board. He commandeered the airplane over Albuquerque, New Mexico, with an empty 22-caliber pistol that he removed from a small white bag. He forced the jet to return to the Los Angeles International Airport, where he agreed to release the crew and passengers only after he was granted his demand to speak over Spanish language radio and television.[61]

On the air, Chavez-Ortiz, who spoke only Spanish, said he wanted nothing for himself, but only to speak out about his own family experience with racism and injustice in Los Angeles. He urged *La Raza* to unite and fight for justice, for an end to racism, and for a better education for all children. He spoke about the injustices suffered by Chicanos, Blacks, Asians, and poor White people in the United States.

He spoke about his personal life, his menial jobs, and the problems of unemployment, low wages, and racial discrimination.

Chavez-Ortiz spoke for 35 minutes, while the FBI stood close by with high powered precision rifles. Presumably, the FBI could have killed him on command while he was still in the grounded jet airplane. At the conclusion of the press conference, he handed the empty gun over to the airplane captain and the FBI took him into custody immediately. A federal judge set bail at $500,000 on a charge of hijacking, which carried a penalty ranging from 20 years to life in prison.

The morning following his arrest, Chicano activists delivered groceries for two days to the large Chavez-Ortiz family. The food was purchased with funds collected in my Chicano Studies classes at nearby Cal State LA. During the day, Spanish language radio stations reported receiving many calls that expressed empathy with Chavez-Ortiz and what he said. At the Queen Mary ship stationed in Long Beach Harbor, 20 Chicano workers who said Chavez-Ortiz inspired them staged a wildcat strike and walked off their jobs to protest low wages and bad working conditions.

On the afternoon of April 14, the court reduced the bail amount, but it was still too high for the family to pay. Two hundred movement activists met that evening at Casa Vecindad in Lincoln Heights to discuss the case and formed a loose umbrella group named *Pobres Unidos de Aztlan*. Its goals were to provide for the legal defense of Chavez-Ortiz, to provide for the needs of his family, and to fight the problems he identified during his speech. Activists from Casa Carnalismo, Casa Hermandad, and *La Raza Unida* joined with Casa Vencidad and created a Ricardo Chavez-Ortiz Defense Fund. They also declared intentions to expand the struggle to include freedom for all Chicano activists, who they termed, "political prisoners."

On April 16, 1972, a Sunday afternoon, over a thousand Chicano movement activists held a protest march in front of the Los Angles County Jail and the Federal Courthouse downtown. A long line of federal marshals stood on security duty on the sidewalk and inside the federal building. But the federal judge took notice of the high Chicano community interest in the case and on April 19, bail for Chavez-Ortiz was reduced to $35,000 -- an amount within range of the defense committee. The following morning, Chavez-Ortiz went home on bail to wait for the final outcome of his daring act.

On Saturday, April 29, Catholic Bishop Juan Arzube celebrated a "Mass of Conscience" with mariachis at St. Alphonsus Catholic Church in East Los Angeles for the spiritual needs of the Chavez-Ortiz family, and to help them gain both strength and humility in this time of crisis.

A group of supporters invited Chavez-Ortiz to speak at East Los Angeles College on May 6, 1972. A small but enthusiastic group welcomed him with applause. Those of us who heard him speak remember his sincere and effortless explanation of his motive for the airplane hijacking. He said he spoke for all families of all races in economic distress, not just for Chicanos. He called for multiracial cooperation to fight injustice. His greatest concern was over the future of school children who were not learning, but succumbing to the lure of drugs and gangs. He urged families to unite to defend their children in the schools and he pleaded with us to change social circumstances. At the end, he said his own sacrifice was a great one to him because it took him away from his wife and family.

In November, Chavez-Ortiz was found guilty of air piracy and given the minimum federal sentence of 20 years in prison.[62] Movement activists understood the private anger and frustration that led Chavez-Ortiz to his dangerous individual protest and imprisonment. He belonged to no political group and acted alone. Yet this tragic and dangerous case added a sense of urgency to the Chicano movement, a stirring that something significant had to be done about the deplorable social conditions of the Mexican American people.

A year later, on April 14, 1973, five hundred activists marched from Indiana Street and Brooklyn Avenue to a rally at Belvedere Park in East Los Angeles to criticize an unjust legal system. They expressed support of political prisoners, including three Chicano activists accused of shooting an undercover federal agent, whom they say they thought was a drug dealer.[63] Activists insisted on justice inside the criminal justice system. The demand for an end to police abuse continued as a movement goal.

Bombs and Fires

During this time of restlessness, rumors spread in Los Angeles about a secret underground group called the Chicano Liberation Front (CLF), said to be involved in a series of unsolved fire bombings in the area. Five buildings were fire bombed, including one at Roosevelt High School and a Board of Education administration building, both in Boyle Heights, and the Bank of America in City Terrace.[64] The rumors of an unknown violent militant group that called itself "Chicano" injected fear and tension into the area. Some people received anonymous threats of harm, but nobody was physically hurt and no suspects were ever arrested. Members of the CLF remained unknown.

On August 6, 1971, the Chicano Liberation Front (CLF) delivered a 12-minute tape-recorded message to the newspaper, Los Angeles Free Press. It claimed responsibility for 28 bombings in Los Angeles between March 1970 and July 1971. The bombings they listed included government buildings, banks, markets, businesses, savings and loan offices, and police cars. CLF claimed credit for the February 1971 theft of 56 M-1 Rifles from the Reserve Officers Training Corps at Lincoln High School in Lincoln Heights. It urged urban guerrilla warfare to fight police terror. The group also blamed what it called lying politicians and greedy businessmen for racist social conditions for which it claimed revolution was the only answer.[65]

Regardless of its hidden identity, acts of violence attributed to the CLF led to loss of support among movement activists opposed to violence. The violence contributed to a public image of the whole movement as violent and unworthy of support. Movement groups nonetheless continued to recruit other activists to work peacefully for justice and against racism. They continued their work to build a positive, nonviolent image of the Chicano movement.

Chapter 8

The Mid-Seventies

Growing Numbers and Women

Mexican Americans entered the mid-seventies with a dramatic increase in population numbers. More than 2.1 million Spanish surnamed native and immigrant persons lived in California, and over a million of them resided in Los Angeles. The state Fair Employment Practices Commission reported that in 10 years, Mexican Americans had increased twice as fast as the total population.[1] But despite increases in population, the situation for Mexican Americans had not improved at all. Almost two-thirds had not completed high school, and most of those employed were in blue collar jobs or worked in one of the trades.

The U.S. Commission On Civil Rights issued a series of reports that gave a national profile of Mexican Americans.[1] Los Angeles attorney Manual Ruiz, Jr. served as a member of the commission at that time. The reports showed that Mexican Americans experienced widespread discrimination in the justice system, ranging from verbal abuse to physical violence. It documented anti-Mexican discrimination in employment, and found that Mexican American students attended substandard schools and received an inferior education.

The same demographic profile applied to Mexican Americans in Los Angeles. Local schools continued to provide inadequate counseling to students, less meaningful curricula, dilapidated school buildings, overcrowding, and some culturally insensitive teachers and administrators. On January 21, 1974, the U.S. Supreme Court rendered its landmark Lau v. Nichols decision that gave movement groups legal grounds to demand better schools. It paved the way for bilingual/bicultural education as a basic right of non-English speaking students. It led to greater implementation of bilingual education programs in Los Angeles and increased professional opportunities for Chicano teachers. The overwhelming dropout rates for Chicano young men and women students, however, continued to remain high.

At the same time, the growing national feminist movement for social justice reached East Los Angeles. Women activists challenged the role of male dominance in the movement, and in social and political life as well. Male leaders traditionally spoke for activist groups and became public spokespersons for movement events. Women activists determined to change that as *La Chicana* emerged as a force in the movement.[3] A large number of women in activist groups began to speak out louder in their own behalf.

Francesca Flores led a group that formed *Comision Femenil* in 1972, which in turn established the Chicana Service Action Center that same year. It provided counseling, job training, and political consciousness to liberate Mexican American women from sexism and racism.[4] In the meantime, MECHA at Cal State LA, held a Chicana Conference that questioned male dominance in the Chicano movement. Vickie Castro, who had been a student activist on campus, became a school teacher after graduation, and later ran for a seat on the Board of the Los Angeles school district. She won.

On April 29, 1972, two hundred women met at a Chicana Conference held at Casa del Mexicano in Boyle Heights. They objected to racial, sexual, social, and economic exploitation of women in society and within the Chicano movement. They raised specific issues important to women, like worker and immigrant rights, welfare and housing rights, Planned Parenthood, and the role of women in the Chicano family.[5]

In the meantime, Alicia Escalante, founder and president of the East Los Angeles Welfare Rights Organization, continued to speak out about injustice to families on welfare and also fought unfair landlords. She joined her group to larger anti-war protests and demands for justice.[6] At the same time, women in the UFW acquired more opportunities in jobs traditionally performed by men, including work as union organizers in the fields.[7]

Labor Pickets

By 1972, some Chicano movement groups began to integrate activities with the larger labor movement. They gave active support to Chicano workers on strike and in labor unions. They supported the strike against the Farah Manufacturing Company in El Paso, led by Chicanos in the Amalgamated Clothing Workers Union. In December, 1972, a thousand movement pickets protested the sale of Farah pants at the May Company and The Broadway stores in downtown Los Angeles.[8] By then, some of the movement activists organized "flying squads" -- small action groups ready to support workers on picket lines -- in selected labor disputes throughout the Los Angeles area.

In the meantime, movement groups increased support for the UFW, especially against the Teamsters Union after they organized a drive in the fields meant to undercut the farmworkers' union. Movement groups helped form picket lines in front of Safeway Stores in Los Angeles to halt the sale of grapes harvested by nonunion workers. The National Conference of Catholic Bishops, the Priests Senate of the Catholic Church in Los Angeles, and Protestant church groups also endorsed the 1974 grape boycott.[9]

Continuing Protest

By 1973, the U.S. declared a cease-fire in Vietnam and the U.S. military draft was suspended. After the war in Vietnam ended, Chicano movement activism in Los Angeles began to slow down, but the movement remained alive with bursts of renewal protests by small groups.

For example, the defense continued of "Los Tres," three young Chicanos from Casa Carnalismo charged with assault on a federal undercover police agent in 1971. The defense committee accused the federal government of trying to pacify the movement with drugs.[10] Los Tres asserted that a federal agent posed as a drug dealer. On May 19, 1973, the defense committee gathered about 1,000 people at Hollenbeck Park in Boyle Heights to express solidarity with the three federal prisoners and reaffirmed its determination to rid the community of drug dealers.[11]

In Lincoln Heights, a new activist group emerged: The Committee To Stop Home Destruction, led by Rosalio Munoz. The group received support from the Center of Metropolitan Mission In Service Training (COMMIT), a group of Protestant churches determined to fight urban renewal. The city's Economic Development Corporation planned to relocate local residents to make room for a 300-room hotel, a theme restaurant, and a shopping center near Lincoln Park.

I joined with other movement activists to assist local residents in opposition to these city plans. We particularly opposed the forced removal of Chicano homeowners, such as was done during the prior removal of Chicano families from Chavez Ravine for the construction of Dodger Stadium.

The Committee To Stop Home Destruction also blocked plans by the city to build unwanted luxury homes in Lincoln Heights.[12] [13] Starting in 1958, the downtown skyline had begun to change. Since then, a large number of buildings over 13 floors had been built. The rising cost of downtown real estate promoted this planned home destruction in order to build new skyscrapers.[14]

Instead of a protest march, the committee took its demands directly to members of the city council and Mayor Sam Yorty. In May, 1973, the group gathered over 800 residents at a special meeting with Mayor-elect Tom Bradley at Lincoln High School. Bradley, who had not yet developed a close relationship with land developers that marked his later years in office, pledged to stop the redevelopment project. The local group victory saved Lincoln Park and its surrounding homes.[15]

Another community fight took place to save Lincoln Park. Back in 1969, residents near Lincoln Park heard that the old boathouse on the lake would be torn down. People had nostalgic feelings about the boathouse. Grandparents told stories of how they met and dated at the park. Families had pictures and memories of wedding parties and day-long picnics at the park. To them, the boathouse was an integral part of Lincoln Park.

Frank S. Lopez organized a small nonprofit corporation, Plaza de La Raza, to restore the boathouse. It convinced city officials to renovate the park instead of demolishing it. Then the group expanded its efforts to improve the entire park. By the mid-seventies, a complex of modern buildings and cultural programs known as Plaza de La Raza reminded park users of cultural pride and perseverance.[16] Plaza de La Raza continues to offer after school programs in the music, dance, visual arts and theatre for children and adults.

Other resident groups resisted large land developers. Residents of the Temple Street-Beaudry Avenue neighborhood, located downtown just west of the Harbor Freeway, provide another example of successful resistance to land developers. Residents fought plans to build a multi-million dollar Bank of America data processing center that would displace 100 Mexican American families from rental housing. The nearby Bunker Hill development project of high priced condominiums and offices had already forced families to move to the Temple-Beaudry area. The area consisted mostly of dilapidated housing, high rents, and immigrant families.

The residents contacted Rosalio Munoz for support. I joined the group of residents for a campaign to fight back. We won city assistance for new housing and a precedent-setting agreement from the private developer to provide major financial support for families required to relocate. The financial support set an example of how the private sector could meet its moral obligation when people are displaced for development projects.[17]

Chicano movement groups continued to defend undocumented Mexican immigrant workers against neighborhood and work site raids and arrest by immigration officers. On June 16, 1973, a coalition of Centro de Accion Autonoma (CASA), Casa Hermandad General de Trabajadores, Casa Carnalismo, MECHA, and La Raza Unida held a protest march against deportations in Los Angeles. About 1,500 people, including some undocumented workers, marched up Broadway Street from Olympic Boulevard to City Hall. The marchers yelled slogans like "Raza Si! Migra No!" along the way. Speakers at the rally denounced the Rodino Bill, restrictive immigration legislation then pending in Congress. They clearly identified the U.S. Immigration and Naturalization Service (INS) as a movement enemy.[18] [19]

The terrorist Symbionese Liberation Army (SLA) began to overshadow publicity of Chicano movement events. On February 4, 1974, the SLA kidnapped newspaper heiress Patricia Hearst from her Berkeley, California apartment. The SLA moved to Los Angeles and dominated news media coverage for a year.

But Chicano movement groups continued to make defense of undocumented immigrant workers a mainstay of Los Angeles politics. They often formed picket lines in front of the downtown federal building and refuted arguments that undocumented workers created unemployment.

Activists demanded full protection of due process under the U.S. Constitution for every person, citizen or not. On August 31, 1974, about 1,000 men and women marched three miles from Belvedere Park to Salazar Park, in East Los Angeles, to protest anti-immigrant legislation and the deportation of undocumented immigrant workers. Marchers also commemorated the fourth anniversary of the August 29, 1970, Chicano Moratorium anti-war march and the death of Ruben Salazar.[20]

Nonetheless, three months later, in November of 1974, U.S. Attorney General William Saxbe announced his intention to deport one million undocumented immigrants the following year. Movement groups promptly denounced Saxbe's plan. They called it a declaration of an open season on all Mexicans and an attempt to scapegoat undocumented immigrants for U.S. economic problems.[21]

Problems of injustice continued and movement groups in turn mobilized in opposition. Some groups took up the name "Chicano Moratorium Committee" and led anniversary marches and commemorations of the August 29, 1970, anti-war march in East Los Angeles. Even up to the 1990's, various groups emphasized familiar concerns of injustice with variations depending on current political circumstances.[22] The Mexican American Political Association (MAPA), the American GI Forum, the League of United Latin American Citizens (LULAC), Comision Femenil, and others gathered periodically for Mexican American Issues Conferences that discussed problems that affected the Mexican American people. In 1974, this is where the demand originated for the resignation of U.S. Attorney General William B. Saxbe after his announced intention to deport one million undocumented Mexican immigrants.[23] Movement groups also joined public demands for the resignation of President Richard Nixon after the Watergate scandal.

In 1974, activists formed a new group called the August 29th Movement (ATM) in East Los Angeles. It added a leftist influence in the overall movement and added energy to movement protest events in response to the police riot.

Artists and Writers Protest

The message of the continuing Chicano movement appeared in art works by men and women that pointed toward themes of new values of justice and liberation.[24] Chicano artists expressed anger and frustration with social circumstances but found hope in struggles for social change. They depicted cultural themes from history and current problems that reflected labor, educational, and political struggles.[25] In 1973, Carmen Zapata founded the Bilingual Foundation of the Arts to involve young

Chicanos in the arts. Ironically, it was located in the old city jail in Lincoln Heights. Chicano art and literature have been proven to have value as imaginative and creative representations of a historical and present people.

Artists like George Yepes and Harry Gamboa also enlivened the Mexican tradition of mural painting. Their murals depict Chicano movement turns of events and focus mostly on "life" in Mexican culture and "death" in the majority U.S. society. They appeared in a series of larger-than-life paintings in vivid colors on walls around neighborhoods, like those sponsored by a beautification project in Estrada Courts in Boyle Heights. They played back Chicano history, religion, culture, and the movement in picture messages about Chicanos as true heroes united in struggle. They reminded local residents of their cultural identity with depictions of Benito Juarez, Emiliano Zapata, Pancho Villa and Aztec warriors.

The movement also became part of the background that gave substance and life to the emerging Chicano theater, which by then had become acknowledged as an art form. El Teatro Campesino, founded by Luis Valdez from among farm workers on strike, created new theatre that combined bilingual drama, humor, Mexican "*corrido*" music, and satire. It inspired social action, explained problems, demeaned enemies, suggested solutions, and reflected a people's perception of social conditions.[26] Chicano theater subsequently led to major play productions like "*La Grande Carpa de Los Rasquachis*," which played to acclaim in New York and Los Angeles in 1974. It also portrayed the modern Chicano experience to general U.S. audiences in plays like "Zoot Suit," which later became a movie, and "La Bamba."

Chicano writers also depicted the movement in different ways that described ethnic pride, culture, history, anger at injustice, and a will to struggle for justice and political power. Militant Chicano lawyer Oscar Acosta, for example, captured a slice of movement life around his own experience in his novel, *The Revolt of the Cockroach People*.[27] Writers and poets collectively recreated Chicano movement images with their focus

97

on life in the barrio, a demon Anglo world, and a liberating identification with and belief in things Chicano, called "*Chicanismo.*"[28]

Sporadic Protest

Activists continued to organize sporadic protest demonstrations for more immediate reasons. Some demanded government funds for agencies that provided jobs. Others went from one protest event to another like restless warriors attracted to the drama and excitement of mass protest. Some simply got tired, frustrated, or became preoccupied with other interests, and as a result stopped active participation in movement events. Some also spent more time on job promotions and advancement in professional careers.[29] Still others began to redefine a liberationist role for Chicanas inside the larger national feminist movement.[30]

By the mid-seventies, clusters of Chicano movement veterans and new recruits continued to pursue an intellectual vanguard role in the political development of the Mexican American people. A strong sense of cultural identity drove some to promote formation of a separate Chicano nation in the U.S. Southwest.[31] Others, equally committed, advocated ultimate reunification of the Mexican people on both sides of the U.S.-Mexico border, while some favored an integrated, multiracial, unified working class struggle for justice in the United States.

A divergence in movement strategy continued in the form of movement loyalists who pursued strict ethnic politics and others who sought multiracial allies. Some Chicano activists criticized the UFW for an insufficient emphasis on Chicano nationalism in its organizing. The UFW, however, persisted in including Anglos, Filipinos, and Blacks in its efforts to reach 3.5 million farm workers in the United States. It regarded a strict emphasis on Chicano nationalism as counterproductive to organizing campaigns in 20 states.[32]

Both strict nationalists and multiracial advocates nonetheless engaged in common battles for more effective Chicano participation in mainstream society. A combined broad spectrum of Chicano movement protest and pressure groups created affirmative action strongholds in government agencies, obtained government funds for community agencies, and opened access to financial resources for Mexican American business firms. The National Council of La Raza (NCLR), founded in 1972 with a national headquarters in Washington D.C., and The East Los Angeles Community Union (TELACU), formed in 1968, served as examples of organizations that lobbied successfully for federal, state, and corporate funds for community service programs.

The number of government-funded community agencies increased while they relied on a strict service approach to community problems. They established a constituency of service recipients who were formed into pressure groups when necessary to secure continued government funding. The Chicano movement as a whole slowly became a cluster of government funded community agencies, support groups, business groups, and professionals. It set in motion a new politics centered mostly on electoral campaigns, interest groups, and pressure groups.

New Electoral Politics

By the mid-seventies, most Mexican American civic groups and movement organizations, especially those attached to government funding, changed Chicano politics in Los Angeles. They evolved into competitive pressure groups in electoral politics. They campaigned hard to elect a new breed of officials who were more accessible to community groups. By then, the drama and rewards of electoral politics captured the imagination of movement groups.

A California Supreme Court decision helped place electoral politics in the center of the Chicano movement. In March 1971, the court ruled in the Calderon Decision, named after plaintiff Richard Calderon, those city councils must reapportion themselves on the basis of "one-man, one-vote," not on the number of registered voters in a district. The court decision led to the creation of a "safe district" for a Chicano candidate for the city council. Chicano office-seekers began a campaign to elect a Chicano to the 15-member Los Angeles City Council. Over 20 percent of the city population was Mexican American, yet no Chicano had served on the city council since 1962, until the election of Richard Alatorre in 1985.

The desire to elect Chicanos to public office was longstanding. Mexican American candidates in the Democratic Party began to overcome racist reapportionment practices that had been identified by the California State Advisory Committee to the U.S. Commission On Civil Rights.[33] Chicanos began slowly to win elective office against protected incumbents over time. Among the Mexican Americans who won election to the state Assembly from East Los Angeles were: John Moreno, Phil Soto, Alex P. Garcia, Richard Alatorre, Art Torres, Gloria Molina, Richard Polanco, Lucille Roybal-Allard, and, more recently, Xavier Beccera, Diane Martinez, Martha M Escutia, and Louis Caldera.

Alatorre and Molina later won seats on the Los Angeles City Council and, in 1991, Molina won election to the Los Angeles County Board of Supervisors and Mike Hernandez was elected to the Los Angeles City Council. In 1993, Richard Alarcon from the San Fernando Valley also won a seat on the city council. Leticia Quezada served on the elected Los Angeles Board of Education. In 1992, Edward R. Roybal retired from the U.S. Congress while his daughter, Roybal-Allard, and Beccera won election to join Esteban Torres and Mathew Martinez in the U.S. Congress.

Together, Mexican American elected officials addressed community concerns more directly and helped expand affirmative action opportunities for businesses and professionals. They raised community expectations for effective power in the democratic process and governance.

Nonetheless, an unusual correlation emerged: the number of community elected officials and poverty went up at the same time, as more unemployed young and adult men and women sought work to support their families.

Poverty and racism in society remained too intractable and beyond easy solutions. Three Mexican Americans on the 15-member

Los Angeles City Council and one on the five-member Los Angeles County Board of Supervisors remained insufficient to promote a strict Mexican American agenda. They had to rely on other elected allies to enact special community-based legislative goals. Electoral victories helped motivate upward mobile, professional career-oriented Mexican Americans to get involved in electoral politics. But a much greater and growing number of Mexican Americans remained trapped in poverty, deteriorated housing, and ineffective schools.

Chicano elected officials slowly expanded their own political spheres of influence. Movement groups remained neighborhood based, but elected officials operated in larger arenas of policy making and ventured past lower levels of state and national politics. They began to reexamine their image as minor lieutenants of more prominent politicians in Sacramento and Washington D.C. To increase their political power, in 1975 they formed their own organization with staff. called the National Association of Latino Elected Officials (NALEO) and led by Congressman Edward R. Roybal of Los Angeles.[34]

Chicano elected officials gradually became the strongest force in Chicano politics, mostly because they were better organized than civic and movement groups. They developed more effective and better funded community-based support groups as they cemented ties with organized labor. This led to new style political machines in Los Angeles and changed Chicano politics. Ready-made campaign supporters came from public workers and employees of government-funded agencies that depended on politicians for support.

While this was happening, Chicano movement groups remained nationalistic, each with a narrower agenda. Activists also had a loose, often spontaneous, method of contact with each other, unlike elected officials whose staff stayed in contact with interested groups. Meanwhile, Chicano elected officials began to play a more prominent role in Chicano politics, with or without support of movement leaders. In essence, Chicano politicians with media publicity became the "rock stars" of Chicano politics.

Changing Economy

Changes in the world economy created a modern context for a new phase in the political development of the Mexican American people. The world economy began to change from an industrial to a service and information economy, which Alvin Toffler described in his book, The Third Wave.[35] Robert Reich also identified changes in the national economy that took place in Los Angeles.[36] Major manufacturing factories changed from high volume production of standard products to providing services for particular consumers. They focused more on specialized knowledge to service those products. The massive economic reordering threatened the short-term stability of working class Mexican American families.

Beginning in 1970, employment opportunities for Mexican American families in manufacturing began to steadily shrink. By 1990, thousands of area jobs were lost in shut down steel plants run by U.S. Steel and Bethlehem Steel; tire plants owned by Uniroyal, Firestone, Goodrich and Goodyear; and automobile production plants operated by Ford, Dodge and General Motors. A sharper two-tier economy placed most Mexican American workers in a class of less skilled and lower paid workers, like in Third World modes of production based on cheap labor. This economic realignment and two-tier work force separated workers into categories of skilled and unskilled, educated and uneducated, middle class and working poor. It recast old problems in new forms. The Los Angeles Times published a prediction by life insurance executives that U.S. cities would experience economic turbulence and social disruption between 1975 and 1995 caused by a downward trend of the industrial era.[37]

The new Chicano electoral politics by itself could not reduce the growing economic inequity. Movement groups, however, became more focused on the drama of electoral campaigns and candidate personalities as a primary route to social justice. They joined electoral campaigns and trusted charismatic candidates to solve problems of unemployment and discrimination.

However, in their seduction by electoral politics, movement activists were unable to consolidate power with a central organization of groups, like the Council of Mexican American Affairs (CMAA) and the Congress of Mexican American United (CMAU) had attempted. They lacked a permanent membership organization of neighborhood people, especially from the working poor. The movement as a whole remained general in character and sufficiently unorganized for independent political power. Thus, Chicano movement activists and groups remained on the outer edges of the political system.

The Chicano movement, however, changed political relationships between Mexican Americans and other groups in society. In addition to becoming an important political voter bloc in local and national campaigns, a growing number of individual Mexican American men and women achieved success in business, government, and the professions. They retained a strong Mexican American identity and carried the struggle forward for effective participation as Mexican Americans in political, educational, scientific, athletic, and professional fields.[38]

Although not identified as movement leaders, successful professional and business men and women began participation as Mexican Americans in an upper tier of social and economic progress. They carried forward the optimism and hope of the Mexican American veterans of World War II. They pushed ahead individually during the heydays of the Chicano movement and offset a recycling of a past racial discrimination. They rejected depictions of the Chicano people as "the oppressed," destined to live in poverty. They constituted and continue to constitute a Mexican American middle class that insists on full civil rights under the U.S. Constitution and the Bill of Rights. They realize that freedom and civil rights would not come out of the blue, but out of serious and disciplined preparation and hard work. While many individuals did not know it, their drive for expanded economic opportunities and civil rights connect them to the goals of the Chicano movement.

Search for Power

As the Chicano movement lost intensity, activists and community residents remained optimistic with a hope for justice in the midst of poverty and inefficient, overcrowded schools.[39] People whose daily lives evolved around family, church, and neighborhood came together in a search for solutions to community problems.

In 1974, Cardinal Timothy Manning and Bishop Juan Arzube looked at East Los Angeles and saw its people unorganized and powerless. They invited the Industrial Areas Foundation (IAF) to form a community organization based on local churches from diverse religious denominations. The Episcopal Church, United Church of Christ, United Presbyterian Church, United Methodist Church, Disciples of Christ, and the Catholic Church showed enough interest to form the United Neighborhoods Organization (UNO). The Campaign For Human Development funded UNO at first when no one else would provide financial support.

Then, in 1976, UNO went public. Led by Larry McNeil and Mike Clemons, it added multi-faith and multiracial collaboration, training and organizing to community strategies for power. It also reached out to labor unions for consolidated political power as it began to build an organization around their churches. I participated in UNO with members of St. Mary's Catholic Church in Boyle Heights under the leadership of organizers Ana Guerrero, Larry Fondation, and Ken Fujimoto. That was where I learned to appreciate the potential power of church-based campaigns for social justice.

Many movement activists were caught off-guard by this church-based initiative. They were suspicious of community organizing unattached to movement groups, political parties, or office seekers. They were irritated by the UNO practice of building an action agenda from its own membership in a "bottom up" process instead of through political ideology. They would have preferred instead that UNO leaders consult movement activists, liberals, and intellectuals for an agenda.

On the other hand, UNO leaders were more interested in creating community power: what it is, how to get it, and how to use it. UNO achieved success with housing development in Bell Gardens, an anti-gang project in Los Angeles, and increased parent participation in area schools. Eventually, however, UNO reorganized and merged into One LA, a larger citywide organization of churches and nonprofit groups. At this time, UNO's successes in local issue campaigns are worth noting and have yet to be recorded.

Thus, different philosophies and strategies towards political power operated at the same time for Mexican Americans. Civic groups like the League of United Latin American Citizens (LULAC), the American GI Forum, the Community Service Organization (CSO), and the Mexican American Political Association (MAPA) remained influential, though unattached to each other. The Mexican American Bar Association, the American Civil Liberties Union (ACLU), and the Mexican American Legal Defense and Education Fund (MALDEF) continued to win important legal victories. Padres Asociados Para Derechos Religiosos Educativos y Sociales (PADRES) and Las Hermanas continued to help Mexican Americans place the religious faith of church members in the daily celebrations of life and the ongoing struggle for justice.

Mexican American professional groups of engineers, accountants, police officers, and other occupations also became active. Mexican American businesses and manufacturing firms formed associations to compete for government grants and loans for businesses. In this way, Chicano movement activists appeared in many different forms.

Chicano electoral politics continued to dominate the time and attention of movement activists. By the end of the 1970's, the government had become the largest single employer of Mexican American workers. It made lobbying by Chicano interest groups more prominent. Mass protest in the streets became less frequent and new groups formed around defense of government workers and employees in government-funded agencies. They forged stronger links to workplaces and unions, politicians and electoral politics.

At the same time, upwardly mobile Chicano men and women became more prominent in community events. But the Chicano movement itself remained general in character, uncoordinated, with no central headquarters. On the positive side, this lack of central leadership and headquarters allowed individual movement groups freedom to move in any direction at any time without obtaining agreement from any other group. A large formal movement organization with rules or regulations would have controlled activist participation in grass-roots events. Movement activists remained free to act on their own perceptions of injustice.

Chapter 9

Towards Representation

In spite of its general uncoordinated character, or perhaps because of it, the Chicano movement achieved notable success.[1] [2] Now a new generation of active Chicanos, who call themselves Mexican Americans or Latinos, works inside the political power structure. They continue to spark the growth of a professional and middle class, and promote a positive cultural identity rooted in the concept that Mexican Americans and Mexican immigrants are a major, permanent historical positive part of U.S. society. They reject the notion that an oppressed people must wait for a pony rider with blazing guns to rescue them. They rekindle the passion of the walkouts and mass protests. This new generation of Mexican Americans form a base for electoral politics aimed at reducing poverty.

Success also comes in the development of Chicano Studies academic departments in colleges and universities; ethnic studies courses in traditional social studies departments; the formation of immigrant defense committees; and in an increased number of Chicanos elected to public office. However, poverty and anti-Mexican racism continue to persist in America, and today, militant protest groups have gone missing.

I recently attended a reunion of older activists that focused mostly on a commitment to social justice and reminiscence of past protest marches. Comments referred mostly to memories of the Chicano Moratorium protest march, but less often on the need for more protest marches against injustice. The absence of an active protest movement against poverty today creates a vacuum in local and national politics.

These days, public officials use the media to promote fear of undocumented Mexican immigrants as job-stealers or drug dealers -- unproductive and costly drains on the economy. This fear sparks strong opposition to the presence of Mexican immigrant families in Republican-controlled states. In Arizona, the governor signed legislation to arrest and deport illegal immigrants. This new law requires police officers to check the legal status of people who "look Mexican" and thus might be in the country illegally.

Republican Party leaders in the U.S. Congress have even called for an amendment to the 14th Amendment of the U.S. Constitution in order to deny "birthright" citizenship to U.S.-born children of undocumented immigrants. Thus, looking like a Mexican or speaking English with a Spanish accent would invite police to demand papers that prove your citizenship. In this way, anti-Mexican racism has become a national hot button issue in U.S. politics and the anti-Mexican immigrant hysteria goes on.

New movement activists in East Los Angeles remain challenged to confront poverty. Fortunately, a good number of Chicanos raised in low-income families have successfully pursued opportunities to advance. That opportunity must now be made available to all others, especially the poor. Too many Chicanos continue to lag behind Americans, in contrast to a growing number of middle class families outside of East Los Angeles.

However, the Chicano working poor -- immigrants, single parents, families, and ordinary people -- do not participate in government decisions that affect their lives. They turn out to vote in low numbers. They attend cultural "meet the candidate" events but then return home and do nothing until invited to the next one. They play out roles in large numbers as spectators or background for whatever new events occur.

But events do not organize communities. Only hard work, boots on the ground, daily long term organizing efforts will bring communities together to make a difference. Trained community residents, even if poor, can become active decision makers and voters. Community leaders can be trained to become acquainted with local families and church leaders to engage in social justice campaigns. Face-to-face conversations with local residents will help identify issues of most concern to them and allow them to find actions they can take to promote a community-building agenda.

A look at census data helps us see the general problem. According to the 2012 U.S. Census Bureau, the City of Los Angeles has a total population of 3,772,486 and the Hispanic population comprises 48.1% of the total. Of all Hispanics, Mexicans make up 33.2%, much more than other Latino group.[3] Overall during 2012, East Los Angeles was and remains 2.3% white, 5.2% Asian, 0.7% Black, and 91.2% Latino. As might be expected from the continuing issues of poverty and poor schools, household income and educational levels remain low, with over two-thirds of households renting instead of owning their homes.[4]

According to a 2010 United Way L.A. poverty report, Los Angeles is in the middle of the worst economic crisis in generations. The county experienced the greatest job loss since the Great Depression and remains extremely high. Extreme poverty affects minorities worse than Whites, with African Americans and Latinos faring worst of all. Those in extreme poverty in L.A. County, by race and ethnicity as categorized by census reports, were 9.3% White (non-Latino), 10.5% Asian, 19.7% African American, and 21.1% Latino.

At the same time, many people were shown in this report to be poor even if they were working. In 2008, more than one in four full-time workers lived below the poverty line. In industries with the highest rates of working poverty, such as leisure and hospitality, laundry services, domestic work, janitorial services, and construction, this is higher than state and national percentages. More than one-third of all workers lived below the poverty line and many full-time workers do not earn enough to make ends meet. In 2009, an estimated 29% of L.A. County's full-time workers earned less than $25,000 per year. The percentage of the population without health insurance increased from 21.7% in 2008 to 22.6% in 2009.[5] As a result, impoverished residents use the emergency health clinic as a last option. Emergency health services for the poor remains a vital social service.

The latest census shows that on the national level, Latinos have the highest rate of poverty.[6] In California, 20.8 percent of all Latinos live below the poverty line. At the national level, more Latino children live in poverty than any other minority group, at a rate of 37.3 percent.[7][8]

Elected officials remain silent about the unspoken problem of poverty and hunger in Los Angeles. The term "institutionalized racism" has been used to excuse officials from taking action as they viewed the problem as something that was nobody's fault; it was just the way things worked. Officials treated the term "poverty" the same way, as something that is just there, with nobody taking responsible for it.

Chicano movement activists did not specifically pinpoint poverty as an issue in the community. They focused on other issues, like opposition to the war in Vietnam. Without a focus on poverty, the plight of low-income families continued in spite of advances in the quality of the schools, the end to the Vietnam War, and watchful eye on police abuse. The movement became vulnerable to absorption by progressives in local electoral politics and larger national peace, labor, and feminist movements.[9]

Popular Movement Ideas

Over time, a new range of definitions, sometimes contradictory, came to represent Chicano movement goals and various proposed actions. The Brown Berets, for example, would continue to struggle based on ethnic identity, but the UFW advocated a multiracial approach towards social justice. Likewise, some movement groups attacked the Democratic Party while others served it. Mexican American candidates won elective office as Democrats chosen to represent the same electorate that was targeted by *La Raza Unida* Party. Thus, movement activists differed on proposed political action depending on individual strategies inside a social situation. Just like in many political actions, factions formed inside the movement but groups were able to form consensus on major events.

Likewise, differences also emerged in strategy towards achieving movement goals. Some groups, like the Mexican American Education Commission, pursued social change from within existing government institutions. Others, like the Brown Berets and the Educational Issues Coordinating Committee (EICC), engaged in protest demonstrations from the outside to create pressure for change. Still other groups, like the courthouse takeover in Tierra Amarilla, engaged in violent confrontation as a last resort. Different groups with members based on what they expect in an action linked up for justice.

Resistance to specific Chicano movement tactics, however, also came from groups inside the movement. This tension explained why *La Raza Unida Party*, for example, faced insurmountable obstacles to become a viable political party. It was unable to persuade enough movement activists and voters to accept an ethnic third party approach to electoral power. Opposition came from established activists in the Democratic and Republican parties and from labor, business, and other activists who disagreed. Despite a cross-current of dynamic dialog on tactics, strategies and what each action was meant to accomplish, most movement activists remained loyal to an established political party and electoral patterns. Old habits died hard, if at all.

Just as important, the failed attempt to convert the Chicano movement into a third political party emphasized the lack of central organization. This in turn allowed movement groups to operate autonomously, based on their own agenda, even if they sometimes cooperated with other groups. The diffusion of movement leadership helped unleash militancy in local groups. They were free to interpret situations differently, even when they shared common regional goals. Absent restraints, there was no need to balance conflicting local demands inside a regional strategy. Unchecked and uncoordinated local movement groups became more combative and militant for social justice, thus alienating the more conservative established organizations.

In this way, the Chicano movement in Los Angeles appeared as a series of social acts in motion, a process of collective action. Its contradictions and ambiguities associated people with each other and in the process gave it diversity, vitality and strength. It appeared as a collective moving ahead rather than as a fixed number of groups, state of events, permanent participants, or fixed ideology. This process of social activism across the usual divisive lines remains essential to effectively fight for justice.

Chapter 10

What Now?

Men and women in the Chicano movement made important contributions to social and economic justice in Los Angeles. The movement expanded participation in democracy for a new generation of Americans. It helped shape dialogue over public policy for quality public schools, fair employment for minorities, and advocacy for fairness for immigrant families. It opened the door for expanded affirmative action in employment opportunities for a previously excluded Spanish-speaking minority. It made a unique contribution to the national anti-war movement as the first U.S. ethnic movement to demand an end to the war in Vietnam. It created opportunities for first experiences in social protest for a whole generation of people. It contributed to the evolution of Latino voting power.

Formation of large voter turnouts in East Los Angeles has not yet been achieved. But in spite of a lack of voting power, the Chicano movement deserves credit for increasing the number of modern middle class and professional community activists who participate in government as part of both the Democratic and Republican parties. In this way, Mexican American activists have become part of the electoral politics controlled by politicians, land developers, and major corporations. Movement activists still face a challenge to recreate themselves as an independent block of voters, like allied labor unions led by Maria Elena Durazo. Chicano activists have yet to develop the capacity to hold politicians accountable for low-performance public schools, unaffordable college education, lack of jobs, poverty, and serious health care problems in East Los Angeles.

Those currently active in the Mexican American community now consist mostly of university students, old-time activists, and government-funded service providers. They articulate the needs of the poor and immigrant families with compassion. At the same time, some activists have become more like mainstream activists in education and the professions.

But they, too, have yet to create a solid bloc of independent voters capable of creating change. Some of the newer activists operate in the upper half of the Mexican American two-tier economy and benefit from upward social mobility. But the masses of Chicano people remain locked in low family income, worsening housing conditions, schools that don't teach, and lack of adequate health care. Defense of undocumented immigrant workers and families remains a top priority that binds old and new activists in social action. The non-profit Coalition For Humane Immigrant Rights of Los Angeles (CHIRLA), formed in 1986, continues the struggle for fair treatment if immigrants.

Those who wish to be effective in creating change in the Mexican American community must learn from the past mistakes made by the earlier activists. Key to this is learning to distinguish between electoral politics and independent community power, between hectic activism and focused community campaigns for power, and between rhetorical victories of angry groups and true life achievement of an organized people of power. Total reliance on elected officials without community demands, regardless of race or ethnicity, does not reduce incidence of hunger, low quality housing, or/ drug related violence in local neighborhoods.

The modern Chicano movement must replant its roots in a "bottom up" process to build consensus for community action. Electoral politics, after all, are controlled by powerful special interests. Activist groups have to now connect with each other to reignite community-wide independent voters. A younger generation of agitators needs to evolve out of our colleges and high schools to solidify a bloc of voters apart from elected officials. Trained teams of independent precinct workers must be organized, including the possibility of a coalition with African American voters. The challenge to eliminate poverty remains enormous and as is the opportunity to reduce it.

A modern movement led by Mexican Americans must become able to transcend hectic activism in the form of busy people who attend endless meetings and hold many press conferences as they speak out against injustice. Hectic activism imposes too much noise and activity on people who do not have the time and energy to devote in this way. They must once again recruit each other to thrive on conflict, controversy, and publicity. Communications options have greatly improved and expanded, and modern activists now have use of computers and smart phones to quickly share information with each other, but they also need the structure created by an identifiable, permanent coalition of movement groups, like the potential of a group like the Congress of Mexican American Unity. This critical deficiency limits the potential of further movement success.

A new Mexican American movement must become an identifiable yet independent force in electoral politics. But to survive as a legitimate voice for social justice, this new force of Chicanos needs to return to visions of democracy and fairness for all people. In this era of increasing inequality across America, activists have to reconnect to the potential power of ordinary people trained to participate independently and directly in democracy. The movement must rededicate itself to fulfill its initial promise of a true democracy where the people govern.

How are they to do this? Activists have a mandate to now reach out to low-wage working families and the poor for "get out the vote" campaigns that are independent of elected officials. Unfortunately, poor people do not vote according to their numbers -- but that is the key that will give them the success they need. Activists have to help the working poor register to vote and help them get to the polls in greater numbers. In this way, they will become involved in the process of their own liberation. The change they seek will probably come about slowly, but with this kind of action, it can and will happen.

This vision of a future for Mexican Americans filled with equality, opportunity, and fairness may seem impossible, but if we don't begin the process of creating this future, nothing will change for our people. The development of a new Chicano voting block independent of both political parties calls for a new, informed, energized generation of agitators for Chicano Power.

The time to change is now. The People to do it are you.

Acknowledgements

I wish to acknowledge the encouragement and support of faculty colleagues in the Department of Chicano Studies at California State University, Los Angeles. In particular, I appreciate the encouragement of Roberto Cantu to finish my writing. My former students Sam Rodriguez, Judith Rodriguez, and Cesar Avalos challenged me when we met to complete my manuscript.

I appreciate the opportunities Rosalio Munoz and other community activists, particularly activist students, who gave me opportunities to participate in various movement events.

I am thankful for the assistance of family, friends, and former students in support of my early writing. I am particularly appreciative of the comments and suggestions in reading early chapters provided by Michael Cervantes, Christy Corral, Gerald Espinosa, Rosalie Gurrola, Rachel Keesecker, Alicia Mackey, Alex Negrete, and Diego Negrete. I appreciate of the support of Yvette Casas, Velia Murillo, and Gloria La Brada for assistance in use of my computer.

A former student gave me the picture on the book cover, but I don't remember his name. I hung it in my university office as a reminder of work to be done.

I also appreciate the suggestion by my dentist, John Chao, who referred me to Libbe HaLevy. Libbe served as my writing coach and editor for the book, with helpful comments and suggestions to finish my manuscript and get it published.

References

Introduction

[1] Garcia, Mario T. and Sal Castro. 2011. Blowout! Sal Castro And The Chicano Struggle For Educational Justice. Chapel Hill: The University of North Carolina Press.
[2] Guzman, Ralph. 1968. Press Release. Emergency Committee For The Student Strike. University of California, Los Angeles.

Chapter 1

[1] Morin, Raul. 1963. Among The Valiant. Los Angeles: Borden
[2] Arroyo, Luis Leobardo. 1978. "La Participacion De Los Chicanos En Sindicatos: La CSI (CIO) En Los Angeles, 1938-1950." Pp. 207-246 in Origenes Del Movemiento Obrero Chicano, edited by J. G. Quinones and L. L. Arroyo, and translated by I. Fraire. Mexico, D. F.: Ediciones Era.
[3] Wollenberg, Charles. 1976. All Deliberate Speed. Segregation And Exclusion In California Schools, 1855-1975. Berkeley: University of California Press.
[4] Tirado, Miquel David. 1970. "Mexican American Political Organization, The Key To Chicano Political Power." Aztlan, Chicano Journal Of The Social Sciences And The Arts. 1:1:53-78.

[5] Grebler, Leo, and Joan W. Moore and Ralph Guzman. 1970. The Mexican American People, The Nation's Second Largest Minority. New York: The Free Press.

[6] Tjerandsen, Carl. 1980. Education For Leadership: A Foundation's Experience. Santa Cruz: Emil Schwarzhaupt Foundation.

[7] Marin, Marguerite. 1991. Social Protest In An Urban Barrio, A Study Of The Chicano Movement, 1966-1974. Lanham: University Press of America.

[8] Acuna, Rodolfo. 1988. Occupied America: A History of Chicanos, 3d.ed. New York: Harper.

[9] Rendon, Armando. 1971. Chicano Manifesto: The History And Aspirations Of The Second Largest Minority in America. New York: Collier-Macmillan.

[10] Munoz, Jr. Carlos. 1989. Youth, Identity, Power: The Chicano Movement. Pp. 154. New York: Verso.

[11] Camarillo, Albert. 1984b. Chicanos In California: A History of Mexican Americans In California. San Francisco: Boyd and Fraser.

[12] Gomez-Quinones, Juan. 1990. Chicano Politics: Reality And Promise, 1940-1990. Albuquerque: University of New Mexico Press.

Chapter 2

No references

Chapter 3

[1] Raigoza, Jaime J.M. 1981."The East Los Angeles Cityhood Measure," Campo Libre, Journal of Chicano Studies. 1:1:1-23.

[2] Martinez, Gilberto. 1973. "East LA--A City?" Los Angeles Free Press. August 24. Pp. 6, 29.

[3] del Olmos, Frank. 1973. "Mexican Americans In Battle Over Incorporating East L.A." Los Angeles Times. August 12. Pt. II, pp. 1, 8.

[4] Jones, Jack. 1972. "New L.A. Antipoverty Unit Replaces EYOA." Los Angeles Times. December 16. Pp. 27.

[5] Los Angeles Times. 1970. "Firms Get Rich In War on Poverty. November 30.

[6] Weaver John D. 1973. El Pueblo Grande. Los Angeles: Ward Ritchie. Pp. 124-125.

[7] Negrete, Louis R. 1967. California's Civil Defense And Natural Disaster Program. Report of the Assembly Interim Committee On Military And Veterans Affairs. California State Assembly. Sacramento. January 3. Pp. 67.

[8] Guerra, Manuel H. 1965. Unpublished Paper. Second Annual Conference On The Education Of Spanish Speaking Children And Youth. Richard Garvey School. South San Gabriel. November 20.

[9] Trout, Narda Z. 1974. "Chicanos Charge Job Bias In School Suit," Los Angeles Times. November 22. Pp. 25.

[10] Galarza, Ernesto. 1964. Merchants Of Labor. Santa Barbara: McNally and Loftin.

[11] Negrete, Louis R. 1982. "Labor Unions And Undocumented Workers." The Borderlands Journal. 6:1:1-10

[12] Clement, Norris. 1977. "U.S.-Mexico Economic Regulations: The Role Of California." Background Paper Prepared For The Department of Chicano Studies, California State University, Los Angeles.

Chapter 4

[1] Chavez, Cesar E. 1973. "The Mexican American And The Church." Pp. 215-218. In Voices: Readings From El Grito, 1967-1973. Edited by O.I. Romano-V. Berkeley: Quinto Sol Publications.

[2] Time. 1969. "The Little Strike That Grew Into La causa." 94:1:16-21.

[3] Beck, Paul. 1966. "Mexican American Walkout Mars U.S. Jobs Conference." Los Angeles Times. March 29. Pp. 3.

[4] Jones, Jack. 1966. "Mexican Americans Vow New Area Unity." Los Angeles Times, April 29. Pp. 13.

[5] Ruiz, Ramon. 1968. "Another Defector From The Gringo World." The New Republic. 159:11.

[6] Calderon, Richard M. 1977. "History Of The First Election Of Dr. Julian Nava." Unpublished Report By The Campaign Director. Los Angeles. March 2.

[7] Acuna, Rodolfo. 1988. Occupied America: A History Of Chicanos. 3d ed. New York: Harper. Pp., 331-332.

[8] Morales, Dionicio. 1967. Testimony On "Equal Opportunity In Training – A Threat Or Promise." Pp. 49-51 in A New Focus On Opportunity: Testimony Presented At The Cabinet Committee Hearings On Mexican American Affairs At El Paso, Texas On October 26-28. Washington D.C.: Inter-Agency Committee On Mexican American Affairs.

[9] Gonzalez, Henry B. 1967. Remarks. Congressional Record. House. June 20. Pp. H7582.

[10] Jensen, Richard J. and John C. Hammerback. 1982. "No Revolutions Without Poets: The Rhetoric of Rodolfo "Corky" Gonzales." The Western Journal Of Speech Communication. 46:72-91.

[11] Los Angeles Times. 1966. "Spanish-American Leads Fight To Regain Old Lands From U.S." April 24. Sec. C, pp. 2.

[12] Blawis, Patricia Bell. 1971. Tijerina And The Land Grants: Mexican Americans In Struggle For Their Heritage. New York: International.

[13] Vigil, Maurillo. 1977. Chicano Politics. Washington D.C.: University Press Of America.

[14] Hammerback, John C. and Richard J. Jensen. 1980. "The Rhetorical Worlds Of Cesar Chavez And Reies Tijerina." The Western Journal Of Speech Communication. 44:166-176.

Chapter 5

[1] Acuna, Rodolfo. 1988. Occupied America: A History Of Chicanos. 3 ed. Pp. 337-338: New York. Harper.
[2] Tessler, Ray. 1968. "The Brown Berets." East Los Angeles News. Pp. 5-7. East Los Angeles College. June.
[3] Sanchez, David. 1970. "Chicano Power Explained." Unpublished Paper. Brown Berets. Los Angeles.
[4] Guzman, Ralph. 1969. "Brown Power: The Gentle Revolutionaries." West Magazine, Los Angeles Times. Pp. 9-14. January 26.
[5] Newsweek, 1970. "Tio Taco Is Dead". 75:26:22-28.
[6] Sandoval, Alicia. 1973. "Entrapment." Los Angeles Free Press. Pp. 25. November 9.
[7] Tijerina, Reies Lopez. 1968. Recorded Remarks. Mexican Americans In The Southwest Conference. University of California, Los Angeles. February 22.
[8] Meagher, Ed. 1973. "The Mellowing Of A Chicano Militant." Pp. 3, 20-21. Los Angeles Times. February 20.
[9] Einstoss, Ron. 1968. "13 Indicted In Disorders at 4 L.A. Schools, Arrests Underway." P. 1. Los Angeles Times. June 2.
[10] Los Angeles Times. 1968. "Cal State President Hits Arrest Method." June 4.
[11] Einstoss, Ron. 1968. "Bail Reduced For 9 In Walkouts At 4 Schools." Los Angeles Times. P. 3. June 4.
[12] Gilliam, Jerry. 1968. "Reagan Names 6 Aides For Minority Problems." Los Angeles Times. June 1.
[13] Marshall, Sue. 1970. "Chicanos March For The Dead." P. 8. Los Angeles Times. August 14.
[14] del Olmo, Frank. 1973. "Exile Ends For Controversial L.A. Teacher." Pt. IV. Pp., 1, 2, 3. Los Angeles Times. November 11.
[15] McCurdy, Jack. 1968. "Response On East Side School Demands Hit." Los Angeles Times. August 4.

[16] Guzman, Ralph. 1969. "Brown Power: The Gentle Revolutionaires." West Magazine. Los Angeles Times. Pp. 9-24. January 26.

[17] del Olmo, Frank. 1973. "Exit Ends For Controversial L.A. Teacher." Pt. IV. Pp. 3. Los Angeles Times. November 11.

[18] Moore, Joan W. and Armida Martinez. 1971. "The Grassroots Challenge To Educational Professionalism In East Los Angeles. Pp. 140-188. In Mexican Americans And Educational Change. Symposium Proceedings, edited by A. Castaneda, M. Ramirez III, C.E. Cortea and M. Barrera. Mexican American Studies Program, University of California Riverside. May21-22.

[19] Munoz, Carlos. 1971. "The Politics of Educational Change in East Los Angeles. Pp. 83-104. In Mexican Americans And Educational Change. Symposium Proceedings, edited by A. Castaneda, M. Ramirez III, C.E. Cortez, and M. Barrera. Mexican American Studies Program. University of California, Riverside. May 21-22.

[20] Gomez-Quinones, Juan.1978. Mexican American Students Por La Raza. The Chicano Student Movement in Southern California 1967-1977. Santa Barbara: Editorial La causa. Times. Pt. 111, Pp. 1. June 1.

[21] Munoz Jr., Carlos. 1989. Youth, Identity, Power: The Chicano Movement. New York: Verso.

[22] Munoz Jr., Carlos. 1984. "The Development Of Chicano Studies, 1968-1981. Pp. 5-18. In Chicano Studies: A Multidisciplinary Approach, edited by E. E. Garcia, F. A. Lomeli, and I. D. Ortiz. New York: Teachers College Press.

[23] Munoz Jr., Carlos. 1989. Youth, Identity, Power: The Chicano Movement. Pp. 134-141. New York: Verso.

Chapter 6

[1] Luce, John B. and Armando Morales. 1968. Testimony At Hearing Before The U.S. Commission On Civil Rights. San Antonio. Texas. Pp. 676-685. Washington D.C.: U.S. Printing Office. December.

[2] Gecas, Victor. 1973. "Self-Conceptions Of Migrant And Settled Mexican Americans." Social Science Quarterly. 54:3:579-595.

[3] Anaya, Rudolfo A. and Francisco Lomeli. 1989. Eds. "El Plan Espiritual De Aztlan." Pp. 1-5 in Aztlan: Essays On The Chicano Homeland. Albuquerque: Academia/El Norte Publications.

[4] Anaya, Rudolfo. 1989. "Aztlan: A Homeland Without Boundaries." Pp. 230-241. In Aztlan: Essays On The Chicano Homeland. Eds. by R. A. Anaya and F. Lomeli. Albuquerque: Academia/El Norte.

[5] Pina, Michael. 1989. "The Archaic, Historical and Mythicized Dimensions Of Aztlan." Pp. 14-48 in Aztlan: Essays On The Chicano Homeland. Eds. by R. A. Anaya and F. Lomeli. Albuquerque: Academia\El Norte Publications.

[6] Los Angeles Times. 1969."Chicano Leader To Give Keynote Talk At 4-Day Conference" Pt. II, pp. 1. April 16.

[7] Salazar, Ruben. 1969. "Chicano Must Be Nationalistic To Last In U.S., Leader Says," Pt. II, pp. 1. Los Angeles Times. April 18.

[8] Hager, Philip. 1970. "Suit Asks Release Of 9 In Class For Retarded." Pp. 30. Los Angeles Times. January 8.

[9] Chandler, John T. and John Plakos. 1969. Spanish-Speaking Pupils Classified As Educable Mentally Retarded. Mexican American Educational Research Project. California State Department of Education. Sacramento. April.

[10] California State Department of Education. 1969. Nuevas Vistas. A Report Of The Second Annual Conference of the California State Department Of Education. Mexican American Educational Research Project. California State Department of Education. Sacramento. April.

[11] Salazar, Ruben. 1969. "Mexican Americans Hit Reports On Education." Pp. 26. Los Angeles Times. April 14.

[12] Salazar, Ruben. 1969. "Reagan Seeks Suggestions From Latins." Pt. 11, pp. 3. Los Angeles Times. April 25.

[13] Einstoss, Ron. 1971. "Undercover Officer Set Biltmore Fire, Attorney Charges." Pt. II, Pp. 1, 7. Los Angeles Times. July 27.

[14] Acosta, Oscar Zeta. 1969. "ELA 13 And Biltmore 6." In La Raza 2:10:2.

[15] Einstoss, Ron. 1971. "Disruption Of Reagan Speech Told At Trial." Pt. B, pp. 5. Los Angeles Times. August 18.

[16] Salazar, Ruben. 1969. "Latins Form Distinct Class, U.S. Aide Says." Pt. II, pp. 2. Los Angeles Times. October 23.

[17] Strahm, Susan K. 1969. Court Reporter. Superior Court of the State of California, County of Santa Clara, Juvenile Division. Honorable Gerald S. Chargin, Judge. Courtroom No. 1. San Jose. September 2.

[18] Salazar, Ruben. 1969. "Judge's Latin Slurs Bring Call For Removal." Los Angeles Times. October 2.

[19] Los Angeles Times. 1969. "A Judge Who Disgraced The Bench." Editorial. Pt. II, pp. 6. October 3.

[20] Salazar, Ruben. 1969. "Nixon To Name L.A. Attorney Head Of U.S. Latin Agency." Pt. II. Pp. 1, 5. Los Angeles Times. April 17.

[21] Salazar, Ruben. 1969. "Complaints May Delay Naming L.A. Man As Nixon Aide." Pp., 3, 28. April 30.

[22] Castillo, Martin G. 1969. Statement in Mexican American News, pp. 3. Newsletter of the Inter-Agency Committee On Mexican American Affairs. Washington D. C. December.

[23] The Sun/El Sol. 1970. "Castillo Appointed Federal Ombudsman." Pp. 1, 5. Houston. April 17.

[24] Greenberg, Carl. 1970. "Mexican Americans Hit Nixon Over Latin Jobs." Pt. II, pp. 2. Los Angeles Times. August 13.

[25] Ramirez, Henry M. 1973. Statement On Opportunities For The Spanish Speaking Before The Subcommittee On Government Operations. House Of Representatives. Cabinet Committee On Opportunities For Spanish Speaking People. Washington D.C. July 23.

[26] Cabinet Committee On Opportunities For Spanish Speaking People. 1974. "Cabinet Committee To Close Doors December 30, 1974. Ends Five Years Of Service To Spanish Speaking." News Release. Washington D.C.

[27] del Olmo, Frank. 1974. "1974: The Year Latins Rediscover Politics." Pp., 26. Los Angeles Times.

[28] Holland, Clifton L. 1974. The Religious Dimension In Hispanic Los Angeles. A Protestant Case Study. Pp. 483-484. South Pasadena: William Carey Library.

[29] Romero, Juan. 1990. "Charisma And Power: An Essay On The History Of PADRES." Pp. 613-1051, U.S. Catholic Historian. 9:1-2

[30] Martinez, Demetria. 1991. "Hermanas' Words And Deeds Shaping New Church." Pp. 6-7. National Catholic Reporter. 28:4.

[31] McNamara, Patrick H. 1973. "Catholicism, Assimilation, And The Chicano Movement: Los Angeles As A Case Study." Pp. 124-130 in Chicanos And Native Americans: The Territorial Minorities, edited by R. O. De La Garza, Z. A. Kruszewski, and T. A. Arciniega. Englewood Cliffs, N.J.: Prentice Hall.

[32] Sandoval, Moises. 1983. "The Church And El Movimiento." Pp. 394-396 in Fronteras: A History Of The Latin American Church In The USA Since 1513, edited by M. Sandoval. San Antonio: Mexican American Cultural Center. October.

[33] Catolicos Por La Raza. 1969. Philosophy. Mimeograph Paper. Los Angeles. November 29.

[34] Los Angeles Times. 1969. "Latin Group Urges Church To Be More Radical." P. 8. December 5.

[35] Tidings. 1970. "Militants Mar Mass." Pp. 1, 3. Supplement. Los Angeles. January.

[36] Tidings, 1970. "Demonstrators Ask Cardinal's Forgiveness." Supplement. January.

[37] Ridenour, Ron E. 1972. "Jail Catholics Who Demanded Money For Poor People." Pp. 2. Los Angeles Free Press. May 12.

[38] Dart, John. 1970. "Baptismal Certificates Burned Outside Church." Pp. 18. Los Angeles Times. September 18.

[39] Mosqueda, Lawrence J. 1986. Chicanos, Catholicism And Political Ideology." Pp. 102-113. New York: University Press of America.

[40] Pulido, Albert L. 1991. "Are You An Emissary Of Jesus Christ?: Justice, The Catholic Church And The Chicano Movement," pp. 17-34 in Explorations In Ethnic Studies. 14:1.

[41] Tidings. 1970. "Mexican Catholics Reject Militants" Pp. 1. Supplement. January.

[42] Los Angeles Times. 1973. "Bar Admits Man Cited In Protest." Pt. II, Pp. 2. April 26.

Chapter 7

[1] Munoz, Rosalio. 1969. Statement Read At Draft Board, Mimeograph Copy. Los Angeles. September 16.

[2] Jaimesan, Pat. 1969. "Rosalio Munoz Begins Hunger Strike." Daily Bruin. UCLA Student Newspaper. Los Angeles. November 13.

[3] Cummings, Ridgely. 1969. "LA Still Below National Average." Pp. 1, 2. Lincoln Heights Bulletin News. Los Angeles. October 2.

[4] Flores, Francisca. 1969. Carta Editorial Newsletter. Los Angeles. October.

[5] Ostrow, Ronald J. 1975. "Army Disclosing Its Role In Plans To Quell Urban Riots." Pp. 1, 14-15. Los Angeles Times. August 26.

[6] Rossa, Delia. 1970. "Chicanos Protest Murder." Pp. 12. Los Angeles Free Press. March 6.

[7] Time Magazine. 1969. "The Little Strike That Grew Into La causa." 94:1:16-21.

[8] Newsweek 1970. "Tio Taco Is Dead." 75:26:22-28.

[9] Los Angeles Free Press. 1970. "Cesar Chavez Jailed." Pp. 2. December 11.

[10] 1Andrade, Ray and Ray Martel. 1970. Position Paper Submitted To The TV And Motion Picture Industry Concerning The Elimination Of Discrimination, Maltreatment, And Job Bias In Broadcast Media Against Chicanos. Justicia. Los Angeles. February 24; revised October 1.Andrade, Ray. 1970. Mimeograph Statement. Justicia. Los Angeles. May.

[11] Adams, Burt. 1973. "Personnel Problems In Model Cities." Pp. 5. Los Angeles Free Press. September 14.

[12] Reinholz, Mary. 1970. "Chanting Chicanos Vigorously Picket Academy Awards." Pp. 1, 5. Los Angeles Free Press. April 10.

[13] Sandoval, Alicia. 1973. "Studio Still Biased." Pp. 25. Los Angeles Free Press. November 2.

[14] Salazar, Ruben. 1970. "Chicanos Long Love Affair With Democratic Party Ends." Pt. II. Pp. 7. Los Angeles Times. May 29.

[15] Munoz Jr., Carlos and Mario Barrera. 1988. "The Chicano Student Movement In California." Pp. 213-235 in Latinos And The Political System, edited by F. C. Garcia. Notre Dame: University of Notre Dame Press.

[16] Koblin, Helen. 1972. "Raul Ruiz Tries For Ballot." Pp. 2 Los Angeles Free Press. August 25.

[17] Ridenour, Ron. 1973. "Chicano Activists Win Court Battle." Pp. 6. Los Angeles Free Press. April 20.

[18] Rand, Steve. 1974. "Bert Corona Of CASA." Pp. 5. Los Angeles Free Press. March 15.

[19] Santillan, Richard. 1973. Pp. 84-87. La Raza Unida. Los Angeles: Tlaquilo.

[20] Ruiz, Raul. 1973. "La Raza Unida Party." La Raza. 1:10:5.

[21] Levitt, Dennis. 1970. "Mini-Riot Aftermath To 6 Chicano Deaths." Pp. 1, 5. Los Angeles Free Press. July 10.

[22] Marshall, Sue. 1970. "Chicanos Protest Massacre." Pp. 8, 9. Los Angeles Free Press. July 17.

[23] 1Marshall, Sue. 1970. "Police Kill Two Innocent Chicanos." Pp. 6. Los Angeles Free Press. July 24.

[24] Marshall, Sue. 1970. "Chicanos March For The Dead." Pp. 8. Los Angeles Free Press. August 14.

[25] Arteaga, Alfred. 1970. "National Chicano Moratorium." Pp. 9. Los Angeles Free Press. August 21.

[26] Conde, Carlos D. 1970. "Eulogy." News. Cabinet Committee On Opportunity For The Spanish Speaking. Washington D. C. Newsletter. 11:8:3

[27] Marshall, Sue. 1970. "Salazar Death Aftermath." Pp. 2. Los Angeles Free Press. September 11.

[28] News. 1970. "A Voice Silenced." Newsletter. Cabinet Committee On Opportunity For The Spanish Speaking. Washington D.C. 2:8.

[29] Salazar, Ruben. 1970. "A Beautiful Sight: The System Working The Way It Should." Los Angeles Times. July 24.

[30] Salazar, Sally. 1990. "Ruben Salazar: el hombre. Pp. 5. La Opinion. Los Angeles. August 29.

[31] Castro, Mike and Frank del Olmo. 1975. Pp. 1, 6. "Newsman Salazar Becomes Legend To Some Latins." Los Angeles Times. September 1.

[32] Marshall, Sue. 1970. "East L.A. Riots, Harassment." Pp. 2. Los Angeles Free Press. November 20.

[33] Weingarten, Steve. 1981. "The Life And Curious Death Of Ruben Salazar." Pp. 1, 4-6. Reader. Los Angeles Free Weakly. August 28.

[34] Morales, Armando. 1971. "Chicano-Police Riots." Pp. 184-202. In Chicanos: Social And Psychological Perspectives, edited by N.N. Wagner and M.J. Haug. St. Louis: C.V. Mosby.

[35] Marshall, Sue. 1970. "Mexican Independence Day. Pp. 3. Los Angeles Free Press. September 25.

[36] Rodriquez, Celia L. 1970. "Barrio Defense Committee Charges Law And Order Officials With Genocide." Regeneracion. 1:8:6.

[37] Shaw, David and Johnny Mosqueda. 1971. "36 Chicanos Held In Window-Breaking Melee Downtown." Pp. 1, B, 26. Los Angeles Free Press. January 10.

[38] Munoz, Rosalio. 1971. "Chicanos And The Police." Pt. II, Pp. 4. Letter To The Editor. Los Angeles Times. January 23.

[39] Rossa, Delia. 1971. "Police Meet Nonviolence With Brutality." Pp. 2. Los Angeles Free Press. January 15.

[40] Rossa, Delia. 1971. "Chicanos Answer Davis." Pp. 2. Los Angeles Free Press. January 29.

[41] del Olmo, Frank. 1971. "Chicano Groups Converging For East L.A. Rally." Pp. B, 32. Los Angeles Times. January 31.

[42] Houston, Paul and Ted Thackrey Jr. 1971. "Man Slain As Violence Erupts In East L.A. After Chicano Rally." Pp. 1, 3, 16. Los Angeles Times. February 1.

[43] Browne, Rick. 1971. "Young Chicano's Death Described." Pp. 3, 7. Los Angeles Times. February, 1.

[44] Torgerson, Dial. 1971. "Chicano Violence Laid To Mob That Ignored Monitors." Pp. 1, 3. Los Angeles Times. February 2.

[45] Los Angeles Times. 1971. "Another Scar To Be Healed." Editorial. Pt. II, Pp. 6. February 2.

[46] Munoz, Rosalio. 1971. "An Interview With Rosalio Munoz." Quoted. Pp. 11. La Gente. UCLA Student Newspaper. Los Angeles. May 31.

[47] Romano, Julio C. 1971. "March Of The Reconquest." Pp. 3. La Gente. UCLA Student Newspaper. Los Angeles. May 17.

[48] Kunkin, Art. 1972. "Chicano Leader Tells Of Starting Violence To Justify Arrests." Pp. 1, 30. Los Angeles Free Press. February 4.

[49] 1del Olmo. Frank. 1975. "Riot-Torn Barrio: 5 Years Later." Pt. II, Pp. 1, 2. Los Angeles Times. September 1.

[50] Castro, Mike. 1974. "Activist Seeks Equity In System." Pt. VI, Pp. 1, 3, 5. Los Angeles Times. February 8.

[51] Salazar, Ruben. 1970. "Don't Make The Bato Loco Go The Way Of The Zoot Suiter." Pt. II, Pp. 2. Los Angeles Times. June 19.

[52] Justicia O! 1970. "Chicanos Head Drive For Penal Reform." Pp. 3. Los Angeles. December.

[53] El Pinto. 1970. Journal Of The Penal-Academic Committee. Held At California Institution For Women. Edited By Felix Gutierrez and Ramon Velarde. July 29.

[54] El Sereno Star. 1970. "Model Cities Appointees Announced." Pp.10. Los Angeles. April 23.

[55] Adams, Burt. 1973. "Personnel Problems In Model Cities." Pp. 5. Los Angeles Free Press. September 14.

[56] Negrete, Louis R. 1973. County Planning In City Terrace. A Survey Of Public Opinion. Report Prepared For The East/Northeast

Committee To Stop Home Destruction. Presented To The Los Angeles Regional Planning Commission. Los Angeles. March 21

[57] Hebert, Ray. 1973. "County Planning Efforts Hit By Angry East L.A. Resident." Pt. II, Pp., 1,3. Los Angeles Times. March 22.

[58] Pardo, Eddie. 1973. "Study Presented To Commission, Little Awareness Found In City Terrace. Pp. 1, 2. Mexican American Sun. Los Angeles. March 22.

[59] Negrete, Louis R. 1977. "La Lucha De La Comunidad Mexicano Por Los Derechos Humanos De Los Trabajadores Emigrantes. Pp. 381-389 in Immigration And Public Policy: Human Rights For Undocumented Workers And Their Families. Edited by A. J. Rios-Bustamante. Chicano Studies Center Publications. University of California, Los Angeles.

[60] Roybal, Edward R. 1970. Quoted In "Roybal Asks Resignation Of FBI Chief Hoover." El Sereno Star. Los Angeles. December 17.

[61] Negrete, Louis R. 1972. "Ricardo Chavez-Ortiz: A Voice In The Barrio." Regeneracion. 2:2:4-6.

[62] del Olmo, Frank. 1972. "Chavez-Ortiz Receives Minimum Of 20 Years." Pp. 3. Los Angeles Times. November 30.

[63] Los Angeles Times. 1973. "500 Join Chicano Protest March." Pt. II, Pp. 5. April 15.

[64] Eastside Journal. 1970. "Bank Hit By Fire Bomb, Blame Arsonists, $30,000 Damage." Pp. 1. Los Angeles. April 23.

[65] Blake, Michael. 1971. "Communiqué From Chicano Liberation Front." Pp. 2. Los Angeles Free Press. August 13.

Chapter 8

[1] Fair Employment Practices Commission. 1976. Californians Of Spanish Surname. Sacramento. June.

[2] U.S. Commission On Civil Rights. 1970. Mexican Americans And The Administration Of Justice In The Southwest. Washington D.C. U.S. Government Printing Office.

1970. Report 1. Ethnic Isolation Of Mexican Americans In The Public Schools Of The Southwest.

1971. Report II. The Unfinished Education: Outcomes For Minorities In The Five Southwest States.

1972. Report III. The Excluded Student: Educational Practices Affecting Mexican Americans In The Southwest.

1974. Report IV. Mexican American Education In Texas: A Function Of Wealth.

1973. Report V. Teachers And Students: Differences In Teacher Interaction With Mexican American And Anglo Students.

1974. Report VI. Towards Quality Education For Mexican Americans.

[3] Blea, Irene I. 1992. La Chicana And The Intersection Of Race, Class, And Gender. New York: Praeger.

[4] Sandoval, Alicia. 1973. "Chicana Liberation." Pp. 25. Los Angeles Free Press. November 30.

[5] Sinberg, Andrea. 1972. "Chicanas And Chicanos: A New Voice Is Heard." Pp. 8. Los Angeles Free Press. May 5.

[6] Pardo, Eddie. 1973. "Welfare Rights: Alicia Escalante." Pp. 1, 2. Eastside Sun. Los Angeles. February 15.

[7] Chrouser, Mary. 1973. "Women Farm Workers Are Power Of Strike." Pp. 1, 4. Los Angeles Free Press. May 4.

[8] Ofari, Earl. 1972. "Chavez: Reagan Has A Commitment To Destroy The Union." Pp. 9. Los Angeles Free Press. October 20.

[9] Rand, Steve. 1974. "Gallo "Exorcised" By UFW." Pp. 2. Los Angeles Free Press. March 1.

[10] Sandoval, Alicia. 1973. "Los Tres Out." Pp. 25. Los Angeles Free Press. November 23.

[11] Rand, Steve. 1973. "Los Tres Del Barrio." Pp. 5. Los Angeles Free Press. May 25.

[12] Negrete, Louis R. 1972. "The Conspiracy Of Outside Control," Report Prepared The East/Northeast Committee To Stop Home Destruction. October.

[13] Munoz, Rosalio. 1974. "Our Moving Barrios." Pp. 29-34 in Action Research In Defense Of The Barrio. Edited by M. Barrera and G. Vialpando. Los Angeles: Aztlan Publications.

[14] Turpin, Dick. 1973. "Upward Bound, Not Outward." Pt. V. Pp. 2. Los Angeles Times. July 29.

[15] Martinez, Gilberto. 1973. "Raping Lincoln Heights." Pp. 13. Los Angeles Free Press. July 6.

[16] Whiteside, Beverlei. 1973. "Mexican Americans Put New Emphasis On Culture In East L.A. Community." Pp. A-6. Los Angeles Herald-Examiner. April 29.

[17] Burleigh, Irv. 1974. "Council Oks Aid Pact On Displaced Families." Pt. II, Pp. 1, 3. Los Angeles Times. October 8.

[18] Palladino, Ralph. 1973. "Rally Protests Deportations." Pp. 3. Los Angeles Free Press. June 15.

[19] Palladino, Ralph. 1973. "600 to 1000 Chicanos Arrested In L.A. By Immigration Every Day." Pp. 22, 34. Los Angeles Free Press. June 22.

[20] Los Angeles Times. 1974. "1,000 Protest Deportations." Pt. II, Pp. 4. September 1

[21] Times Advocate. 1974. "Deportation Of Illegal Aliens Scored." Pp. A-3. Escondido. November 8.

[22] Ramos, Lydia and Monica Rodriguez. 1990. "Peace March Recalls Tragic 1970 Protest." Pp. B1, B5. Los Angeles Times. August 26.

[23] del Olmo, Frank. 1974. "Chicano Activists Ask Ford To Seek Saxbe's Resignation." Pp. 3, 21. Los Angeles Times. November 18.

[24] Monteverde, Mildred. 1971. "Contemporary Chicano Art." Aztlan, Chicano Journal Of The Social Sciences And The Arts. 2:2:51-61.

[25] Nevarez, Joe R. 1974. "Chicano Art Blooms In Barrio Warehouse." Pp. 32. Los Angeles Times. December 26.

[26] Pottlitzer, Joanne. 1988. Hispanic Theater In The United States. Pp. 16-24. New York: Ford Foundation.

[27] Oscar Zeta. 1973. The Revolt Of The Cockroach People. San Francisco: Straight Arrow.

[28] Sedano, Michael Victor. 1980. "Chicanismo: A Rhetorical Analysis Of Themes And Images Of Selected Poetry From The Chicano Movement." The Western Journal Of Speech Communication. 44:177-190.

[29] Hernandez, Marita. 1983. "Chicano Movement" A Generation In Search Of Its Legacy." Pp. 1. Los Angeles Times. August 14.

[30] Gonzales, Sylvia. 1975. "What Do Chicanas Have To Gain? What Help Do Anglos Give US?" Pt. II, Pp. 5. Los Angeles Times. September 15.

[31] Barrera, Mario. 1988. Beyond Aztlan: Ethnic Autonomy In Comparative Perspective. New York: Praeger.

[32] Ofari, Earl. 1972. "Chavez: Reagan Has A Commitment To Destroy The Union." Los Angeles Free Press. Pp. 4. October 20.

[33] California State Advisory Commission To The U.S. Commission On Civil Rights.
1971. Political Participation Of Mexican Americans In California. Los Angeles. August.

[34] del Olmo. Frank. 1975. "Roybal Heads New Latin Action Group." Pp. 35. Los Angeles Times. December 14.

[35] Toffler, Alvin. 1980. The Third Wave. New York: Morrow.

[36] Reich, Robert B. 1991. The Work Of Nations: Preparing Ourselves For 21th Century Capitalism. New York: Alfred A. Knopf.

[37] Los Angeles Times. 1975. "Social, Economic Disruption Forecast." Pp. 19. December 22.

[38] del Pinal, Mauricio. 1975. Who's Who In The Latin World. Los Angeles, California. Los Angeles: Tribal Publications.

[39] Gottschalk Jr., Earl C. 1975. "The Chicano "Barrio" Of East Los Angeles Mixes Joy And Despair." Pp. 1, 20. Wall Street Journal. August 8.

Chapter 9

[1] Chavez, Ernesto. 2002. "Mi Raza Primero!" (My People First!) Nationalism, Identity, and Insurgency in the Chicano Movement in Los Angeles. 1966-1978. Berkeley: University of California Press.

[2] Rosen, Gerald. 1973. "Development Of The Chicano Movement In Los Angeles From 1967 To 1969." Pp. 157-158. Aztlan. Chicano Journal Of The Social Sciences And The Arts. 4:1:155-183.

[3] U.S Census Bureau. 2012 ACS Demographic And Household Estimates. 2006-2010.
American Community Survey 5 Year Estimates. Washington D.C. February 29.

[4] Los Angeles Times. 2012. Eastside Mapping 2010 L.A. Census.

[5] United Way. 2010. The Great Recession and Poverty in L.A, County. September 26.

[6] Pew Research Hispanic Trends Project, Hispanic Poverty Rates Highest In New Supplement Census Measure, 2011.

[7] Pew Research Hispanic Trends Project, Childhood Poverty Among Hispanics Sets Record, Leads Nation. 2011.

[8] American Community Survey Briefs, Poverty Rates for Selected Detailed Race and Hispanic Groups by State and Place, 2007-2011, 2013.

Chapter 10

No references

CPSIA information can be obtained
at www.ICGtesting.com
Printed in the USA
LVHW021453301122
734273LV00004B/711